A
CROSS-
SHATTERED
CHURCH

A CROSS-SHATTERED CHURCH

Reclaiming the Theological Heart of Preaching

STANLEY HAUERWAS

BrazosPress

a division of Baker Publishing Group
Grand Rapids, Michigan

Published by Brazos Press
a division of Baker Publishing Group
P.O. Box 6287, Grand Rapids, MI 49516-6287
www.brazospress.com

Printed in the United States of America

Library of Congress Cataloging-in-Publication Data
Hauerwas, Stanley, 1940–
    A cross-shattered church : reclaiming the theological heart of preaching / Stanley
Hauerwas.
        p.   cm.
    Includes bibliographical references (p.   ) and index.
    ISBN 978-1-58743-258-3 (pbk.)
    1. Sermons, American—21st century. 2. Postmodern theology—Sermons. I. Title.
BV4253.H38 2009
252—dc22   2009007345

To
Javier Martinez
Archbishop of Granada
and
William Willimon
Bishop of North Alabama

Contents

Preface

Collections of sermons are seldom best sellers. Even if they are bought they often go unread. That should make anyone think twice about publishing their sermons. I have thought twice about publishing these sermons, but I still think they are some of my best work and I hope they will be widely read. I hope these sermons will be widely read because, for better or worse, they are my determined attempts to show that sermons can develop strong theological claims and yet be existentially compelling.

Cross-Shattered Church, as well as *Cross-Shattered Christ, Disrupting Time*, and most recently the commentary on *Matthew*, are books that I consider to be my most important work. I write a great deal. I ask much of anyone who would read and understand what I have been about. But if you can only read a little Hauerwas, read one of these books. They are what I most care about.

I am indebted to Adam Hollowell for reading through these sermons and for helping put the book together. Carole Baker has been there from the beginning, which means she has responded to earlier drafts of the sermons and made wonderful suggestions for making them better. My wife, Paula Gilbert, has not only read these sermons but has also listened to most of them. Paula claims not to be a theologian, but without fail she makes astute comments that help me say what I was trying to say but would not have known how to without her help. To preach when

Paula celebrates, which was true for several of these sermons, is a privilege for which I am deeply grateful.

I am extremely grateful to Alonzo McDonald and the Agape Foundation for supporting the sabbatical that allowed me the time to put this book together. Al, a former marine, believes theology should matter. He is even willing to support a theologian who is a pacifist because he thinks theology matters. What a gift.

The book is dedicated to two bishops. Will Willimon is the Methodist bishop of North Alabama. Javier Martinez is the Roman Catholic archbishop of Granada, Spain. Will Willimon is an old friend and is one of the best preachers of our day. Archbishop Martinez is a new friend who graciously hosted a conference in Granada in September 2005 to explore the developing theological agenda of John Milbank's and my work. Every morning began with the archbishop saying mass and preaching. Paula and I were often moved to tears by Bishop Martinez's sermons as well as his pain that we could not share the Eucharist. But we could share the Word. I dedicate this book to these bishops, whose office is the office of unity, in the hope that through the faithful preaching of the Word we will be united at the table prepared for us by Jesus.

Introduction

I am a theologian. I am a modern theologian. Modern theologians are primarily at home in the modern university. Accordingly they write primarily for other theologians. Theologians may care about the church, but they do not assume that their most attentive readers should be ministers or laypeople. That most theologians teach in seminaries may seem to belie these generalizations, but even those who teach in seminaries write primarily for those in their professional guilds. The guilds, moreover, are shaped by the expectations of the disciplinary standards of the university.[1]

Because modern theologians are first and foremost academics they tend to spend their lives saying why it is very difficult to do theology in modernity. As a result modern theology tends to be an extended exercise is throat clearing. But even after the theologians have cleared their throats it often turns out they have nothing to say. That is, they have little to say except to say that it is very hard to do theology in modernity.

And it *is* hard to do theology in modernity. But it has always been hard to do theology at any time. There are good reasons to exercise caution when speaking of God. From the beginning the theologians of the church have insisted that we know better what God is not than we know what God is. That our God is to be found in the belly of Mary is

11

surely sufficient to make you think twice that you know what you say when you say "God."

Yet I am determined to do the work of theology. I was raised a brick-layer. Bricklayers work. At the end of the day we like to get down from the scaffold to see what we have done. I confess I have never gotten the satisfaction from any essay or book I have written in theology compa-rable to the sense of accomplishment that comes from a well-laid wall, in which the bed joints are uniform and the head joints true. I assume that is the way it should be because the work of theology should never be finished.

I have, however, increasingly come to the recognition that one of the most satisfying contexts for doing the work of theology is in sermons. That should not be surprising because throughout Christian history, at least until recently, the sermon was one of the primary places in which the work of theology was done. For the work of theology is first and foremost to exposit Scripture. That modern theology has become less and less scriptural, that modern theology has often tried to appear as a form of philosophy, is but an indication of its alienation from its proper work.

I am, therefore, making these sermons available not only because I think they are my best theological work, but because I hope they ex-emplify the work of theology. Of course to suggest that these sermons are unrelenting exercises in theology may deter some. Theology intimi-dates many because theology is associated with esoteric language and reflection designed not to be understood by the uninitiated. I hope the reader of these sermons will find the language accessible not because I try to avoid technical language but because the language I use is the language with which I think.[2]

Yet these sermons are theological through and through. I make no apology for the theological agenda these sermons hopefully exemplify because I am convinced that the recovery of the sermon as the context for theological reflection is crucial if Christians are to negotiate the world in which we find ourselves. I hope the reader will discover that the problem is not that they do not understand what I say. Rather the primary challenge is how what I say challenges the way our lives are put together.

I need, however, to counter a presumption I may have created by suggesting these sermons are my attempt to do the work of theology. It may be assumed the theology that is at work is "my" theology. Of course the theology the sermons exemplify is mine, but the possessive adjective does not mean that the theological perspective I represent is unique to me. The way these sermons hopefully submit to the words of Scripture should remind us that the words of the sermon are not "mine" or "ours." Put differently, I think it a mistake, and it is a mistake often made in recent theology, if theology comes to mean a position taken by an individual thinker. Theologians are not "thinkers." We are servants of a tradition in which the creative challenge is how to be faithful to what we have received.

I do, of course, have strong views. I am, for example, an advocate of Christian nonviolence. I try never to use the sermon to convince those who must hear the sermon that they should agree with, for example, my understanding of Christian nonviolence. I do think that Christians should disavow war, but because I am committed to nonviolence I cannot use the sermon as a stick to beat those who do not believe war is incompatible with the worship of Jesus into submission. Rather my task is to help us discover that through our participation in the proclamation of the gospel we are engrafted into God's peace.

Sermons are an ongoing exercise in what might be called the politics of speech. I have nothing but sympathy for those who must Sunday after Sunday try to negotiate the politics of preaching faithfully and truthfully to a congregation that, for example, assumes that "faith has nothing to do with politics." To counter such a presumption from the pulpit is not easily done. In some small way I hope my attempt in these sermons to reclaim the theological heart of preaching may provide an example of what a theological politics might look like.

In the preface to the collection of Karl Barth's sermons to the prisoners in the Basel prison, entitled *Deliverance to the Captives*, John Marsh observes that many confronted by Barth's theology have wondered, "How does this theology preach?" Marsh argues, however, that Barth would have thought such a question ill formed. It is so because Barth thought theology to be a tool through which we make clear to ourselves and the world the implications of the content of our preaching. Marsh, therefore, suggests a better question: "What sort of preaching lies behind this kind of theology?"[3]

I wish to invite no comparison with Barth, but I hope these sermons exemplify the kind of preaching that lies behind the way I have tried to do theology. I cannot, however, deny that the way I have tried to do theology I learned from Barth. Marsh characterizes that "way" of doing theology as the attempt "to leave completely undistorted and uncompromised the great, wonderful and mysterious fact that God has spoken to us in his Son, Jesus Christ our Lord."[4] I should like to think that sentence also characterizes the way I have tried to do theology.

It is, however, not easy "to leave completely undistorted and uncompromised" the passages from Scripture that authorize the sermon. We, particularly in modernity, have an undeniable desire to explain.[5] Yet that is what I resolutely try to avoid in these sermons. Explanations usually involve the attempt to "get behind" the text to tell us what it "really meant" to those who first wrote or heard what is now reported in the Bible. I have no reason to object to the attempt by historians to reconstruct the text, but I think it a philosophical mistake to assume that by so doing we understand better what the text "meant" or should "mean."

I try to avoid the troublesome notion of "translation" in the way I do theology in these sermons. The assumption that we need to translate the words of the faith into a different idiom because they are no longer meaningful to modern people I fear betrays our unwillingness to live lives required by what we say. I do not think the gospel needs to be demythologized, nor do I develop anthropological accounts meant to show how Scripture confirms what it might mean to be an authentic human being. I do not take as my task to show or explain how the text confirms what we already know, but rather I try to show how the text "explains" our desire to be in control.

I fear that attempts to "explain" or "translate" Scripture too often manifest our attempt to make God conform to our needs. Of course God does love us, but his love usually challenges the presumption that we know what we need. The presumption that the gospel is "all about us" too often leads us to think "good" sermons are those "I got something out of." But sermons, at least if they are faithful to Scripture, are not about us—they are about God. That a sermon should direct our attention to God does not preclude that we should "get something out of it." But you will have an indication that what you got may be true if you are frightened by what you have heard.

I think we look for explanations because we have lost confidence that the language of the faith can do any significant work. For example, I have heard Christians say, "I believe Jesus is Lord, but that is just my personal opinion." What has happened to produce that peculiar speech act? According to Charles Taylor, what has happened is we have moved from a time and a society in which "belief in God is unchallenged and, indeed, unproblematic, to one in which it is understood to be one option among others, and frequently not the easiest to embrace."[6]

If Taylor is right, and I think he is, the situation in which we find ourselves as Christians is at once a threat and an opportunity. For if you believe as I do that there is an inevitable tension between church and world, then a world in which belief in God is unchallenged may be one in which Christians too readily assume that they can be at home in this world. So the world in which we find ourselves may be one in which we recover the difference being a Christian should make. However, in a world in which Christians have lost the sources that make our lives intelligible, we may find ourselves unable to sustain the habits and disciplines—habits and disciplines as simple and as hard as being able speakers and hearers of the language of the faith—necessary to be a people capable of being an alternative to the world.

The world in which we find ourselves as Christians is not unlike the account Jonathan Lear provides of what happened to the Crow in his book *Radical Hope: Ethics in the Face of Cultural Devastation*.[7] Lear's book is centered on the last great chief of the Crow, Plenty Coups, who helped the Crow survive the loss of their way of life caused by the arrival of the white man. The life of the Crow had been centered on buffalo hunting and intertribal warfare. That way of life was lost after the Crow were forced to live on the reservation. That meant, according to Plenty Coups, that the Crow no longer had a story to tell. As he told an interviewer, characterizing his life after the white man, "You know that part of my life as well as I do. You saw what happened to us when the buffalo went away. . . . The hearts of my people fell to the ground, and they could not lift them up again. After this nothing happened. There was little singing anywhere."[8]

"After this nothing happened." Lear, a philosopher as well as a psychotherapist, reflects on this statement. What might it mean? "It would seem," Lear says, "to be the retrospective declaration that history has come to an end. But what could it mean for history to exhaust itself?"[9] Lear's answer to this question, an answer that draws on the philosopher Ludwig Wittgenstein, involves a careful exploration of what a "happening" is. We are able to distinguish one event from another by telling a story shaped by concepts that depend on the lives people live. When the Crow lost their way of life their lives became unintelligible. Thus the poignant experience of Pretty Shield, a Crow woman on the reservation, who observed, "I am trying to live a life I do not understand."[10]

I suspect many of us who count ourselves as Christians share Pretty Shield's understanding of her situation. As Christians we seem to be living lives we do not understand. Sermons are crucial if we are to recover the stories that make it possible to recover Christian practical reason. Put differently, I try to use sermons to develop imaginative skills to help us see the world as judged and redeemed by Christ. For I believe that story has not come to an end, but rather it is a story that makes possible our ability to live lives we do understand—at least if we do not forget that "understanding" does not mean "we have got it all figured out." Sermons, therefore, should help us locate our lives, especially the incoherence of our lives, in God's story.

The story that makes the sermon necessary means the sermon and the story are inseparable. The story that makes us Christians cannot be known without proclamation. Proclamation is a practice constitutive of the story. That is why our task is not to explain "the meaning" of the text, but rather to show how our lives are unintelligible if Jesus Christ is not the Lord.

We need not fear the incoherence of our lives. In the book of Hebrews 2:8–9 we are told, "As it is, we do not yet see everything in subjection to him. But we do see Jesus, who for a little while was made lower than the angels, now crowned with glory and honor because of the suffering of death, so that by the grace of God he might taste death for everyone." I hope the reader will find that this claim is the animating conviction that shapes these sermons. I do not pretend to "have all the answers," but I do maintain that whatever answers we may have should be ones made possible because we do see Jesus.[11]

The refusal to explain does not mean that what we believe as Christians cannot be rationally defended. The alternative to explanation is showing connections and, in particular, the connections Scripture requires and makes possible. Scripture is not self-interpreting. Much of the work of theology involves helping us to develop and remember the reading skills necessary to avoid isolating one part of Scripture from the rest.

What we call Christian doctrine is crucial for helping us see the connections necessary for the story of the faith to be told in all its complexity. Learning to see the connections between the affirmation of the Trinity and the incarnation helps us better understand not only how the story works, but also how the story works to help us see all that is as God's good creation. This is a never-ending task because God's good creation is not finished.

The work of theology, the work at the heart of faithful preaching, is, in the words of John Howard Yoder, "working with words in the light of faith."[12] If such work is done well the hearer or reader of the sermon should think, "That rings true." Recognizing that what is said "rings true" means that what is said can be identified as an honest expression of life's complexities. The challenge is to show that the theological claims, the words that must be used to speak of God, are necessary if what is said speaks honestly of the complexities of life. The worst betrayal of the task of theology comes when the theologian or preacher fears that the words they use are not necessary because the church is no longer understood to be necessary for a relationship with God. The result too often is to confuse sermonizing with entertainment or bombast.

Of course our words are inadequate because we must speak of God, and the God to whom and about whom we must speak defies the words we use. This defiance seems odd because the God about whom we must speak is, we believe, found decisively in Jesus of Nazareth, very God and very man. Yet it seems the closer God draws to us, the closer we are drawn to God by the Holy Spirit, the more difficult it becomes for us to know what we say when we say "God."

Yet speak we must. Which means, according to Yoder, theological work has a double function: (1) to transmit the heritage of the faith without deforming it; and (2) to speak to questions that arise in a new context.[13] There will always be, however, a new context, not only because the world cannot be kept still, but because the very character of God requires that those who worship God be witnesses. Yoder, therefore, argues that the missionary character of the church means that the testing of words, a testing in which sermons play an essential role, can never be over. Rather the words we use, the relation between the words we use, the character of the speaker who uses the words, must be continually tested for their faithfulness to the message of Jesus.[14]

As I suggested above, the pathos of modern theology and preaching has been a loss of confidence in the language of faith. Yoder describes such a loss of confidence as the recognition that no adequate dictionary of the faith exists that might insure us that there is one correct language of the faith. Yet that kind of dictionary, in spite of what many have thought, has never existed. That is why Yoder argues that rather than despair that no such language seems to exist, we should rejoice that God has chosen to use our human weakness, including the weakness of our linguistic and literary tools, for God's purposes. For, as Yoder puts it, whatever the philosophical inadequacy of language as a tool may be, "there still remains the historic usefulness and indispensability of language as a tool."[15] It is the happy work of the theologian and preacher to learn to work with, indeed to learn to play with, the linguistic tools we have been given. Our basic task is word care.

I suspect that the deepest enemy of truthful preaching in our time is not only the loss of confidence in the words we have been given, but also the lack of trust many who preach have that God will show up in the words we use. It is often observed that Methodist Eucharistic practice and thought can be characterized by the belief in the "real absence." Yet

God must be "really present" in the sermon just as God is present in the body and blood of the Eucharist. If God is not so present, then the sermon is but another "talk."

And when a sermon is thought to be no more than a speech by the minister to provide advice to help us negotiate life, the content of sermons usually are exemplifications of the superficial and sentimental pieties of a liberal culture. Then we wonder why the mainstream church is dying. Why do you need to come to church to be told that we ought to treat everyone with dignity? Why do you need to come to church to be told we ought to share some of what we have with those who do not have as much as we have? Why do you need to come to church to be told that children say the darndest things? Why do you need to come to church to hear stories that give us insight into the human condition?

I suspect preachers fall into these familiar traps because not only do we not expect God to show up, but we also do not trust those to whom we preach. God knows we all want to be liked. We want to preach sermons the congregation will "like." Moreover it is hard to preach the truth to those one has come to love.[16] But the truth of the gospel is a harsh and dreadful truth. It is a truth through which we come to recognize that when all is said and done we are sinners who would prefer to live as if God does not exist.

A harsh judgment but one I believe to be true. The violent world we inhabit is killing us. By "we" I mean "Christians." We literally have become murderers in the name of "causes," in the name of "freedom," but the causes and freedom that lead us to kill are not governed by the gospel. And so our violence, even violence enacted for a "good cause," makes us unable to understand the lives we live.[17]

The proclamation of the gospel, the gift of preaching, is crucial if we are to recover the ability to live lives we, as Christians, understand. Accordingly I try to do the work of theology in sermons by showing how the unintelligibility of our lives can be made intelligible by the gospel. My hope is that we will better understand why we live lives we too often do not understand, and see we are not fated to live such lives.

The title of this book, *Cross-Shattered Church*, is obviously a play on the title of my previous book, *Cross-Shattered Christ*. *Cross-Shattered*

Christ collects my sermons on the seven last words of Jesus. Many feel those words, words of agony and hope, describe the state of the church in our day. We are a confused church, but our confusion does not make us "cross-shattered." Rather our confusion is the result of our failure to be a cross-shattered church. It is my hope that these sermons gesture toward what it might mean for us to be a church shaped by the cross of Christ.

In a wonderful article on prayer, Marilyn Chandler McEntyre observes that the scattered, shattered body of Christ, a shifting, rumbling body that is to be found in the many corners of this world, will not be united by means of conferences and negotiations. Our longing for unity means we must participate in conferences and negotiations, but she rightly suggests that only as our bodies are held in common through prayer and Eucharist will we discover the unity that comes through learning to live in dependence on God.[18] McEntyre rightly directs our attention to prayer and Eucharist as crucial for our becoming for the world a cross-shattered church. Yet, as I hope the sermons in this book in some small way suggest, through the faithful proclamation of God's Word we will discover the wounds we share, making our unity in Christ a reality.

That I am given the opportunity to preach is a great gift. I do not take it lightly. I am sure I spend much more time writing a sermon than most of the essays or books I write. I do so because it is my conviction that sermons are more important, that I am under quite a different obligation when I preach than when I write an article or book. Of course I should like to think that the work I do in articles and books informs my sermonic work. Even more important, I hope that what I learn by preaching shapes the way I write in other venues.

There is, moreover, the problem of my ecclesial status. I am not ordained. And, as I suggested above, being a theologian in our day does not mean that you should be trusted with God's Word. I am extremely grateful, therefore, that I am judged worthy and trusted by appropriate authorities to preach. I am particularly grateful to Father Timothy Kimbrough, the rector of the Church of the Holy Family (Episcopal), for inviting me to preach at Holy Family. Father Timothy is a wonderful preacher, which makes his willingness to share the pulpit at Holy Family all the more impressive.

I am also asked to preach in the Divinity School by our chaplain, Sally Bates. Since I am on the faculty it may seem that preaching in the Divinity School might be more "natural." Yet I remain deeply grateful to be given the opportunity to preach to students and colleagues. Some may think that preaching in such a context means the sermon can be more ambitious than in a "normal" congregation. All I can say is that I do think differently when I preach at the Divinity School than when I preach at Holy Family.

Some of these sermons were written and delivered because friends asked me to preach for special occasions such as baptisms, marriages, and to celebrate an ordination. I am a committed lectionary preacher so, unless those being married choose different texts than those appointed for the day, I try to use the texts of the day to shape what it is we do when we baptize, marry, and ordain.

I do try to keep in mind the context of the sermon. Sermons are first and foremost an oral art. Yet, for me, writing the sermon is all important. I write and rewrite, which means, as my wife tells me, my sermons are "tight." I do not think she means that as a criticism, but rather that you have to listen closely because these sermons are arguments. If you miss an early move you may miss the "point." Put differently, because I resist the sermon having *a* "point," I do expect my hearers to do the work of hard listening. Because I think sermons should be arguments, I hope many of those who hear my sermons will also want to read them.

The oral character of sermons or, more important, the liturgical setting for sermons, raises an interesting question: are sermons still sermons when they are collected in a book such as this one? I have no reason to argue that they should be understood as such. They may be better understood, to use John Howard Yoder's description of the essays in his book *He Came Preaching Peace*, as "biblical lectures." A biblical lecture, according to Yoder, is an exposition of scriptural texts in a straightforward manner with an educational purpose.[19] I should be happy for any reader to regard these sermons as "biblical lectures" even though I have no illusion that they are as substantive as the "biblical lectures" produced by Yoder's extraordinary ability to exposit the Scripture.

I have not revised these sermons to free them from the circumstance in which they were written. That they were written for a specific time and occasion does not, in my estimation, present any obstacle to understanding them. What I hope is the case, however, is that by collecting the sermons in one place the reader will begin to see connections between the sermons that strengthen them individually. I am a theologian. I cannot help but think about what I think needs to be said in the sermon I am currently working on in the light of a sermon I have preached in the past.

I have grouped the sermons under the broad categories of "Seeing," "Saying," "Living," and "Events," but I will not be offended by any reader who finds this way of grouping the sermons to be arbitrary. Indeed I invite some to play the game of why, for example, "Witness" would have been better located with the sermons in "Saying." Yet I do hope the way I have organized the sermons helps the reader see as well as make the connections between the sermons that I hope is there. True, if I want the reader to make those connections it means I should not say in this introduction what I hope they will find. But I cannot resist at least alerting the reader to the importance of beauty for understanding the way the words work.

And I should at least make explicit the broad outline of the argument I try to make through these sermons. I wrote "Blinded by the Light" after I had written "Believing Is Seeing" as well as "So Much Depends," but the latter sermons depend on the argument I developed in "Blinded by the Light." These sermons exemplify a theme that has been at the heart of the way I have tried to do theology, that is, with the acknowledgement that we can only act in the world we can see—but we can only see by learning to say. We cannot see the truth about ourselves or the world just by looking. Seeing requires a training through words that transforms our very being. That "doubting Thomas" and the man born blind come not only to see Jesus but also to worship him, I take to be the necessary condition for seeing ourselves and the world truthfully.

"Witness" could be understood as a footnote to these first three sermons. It is so because in it I make candid the presumption at the heart of the sermons on the training necessary if one is to learn to see. That presumption is quite simply that the gospel is not a "truth" that can be known without witnesses. To be sure, Jesus is the Logos, the Second Person of the Trinity, but we know him only through witnesses. There is, therefore, no getting around the contingent character of what we believe as Christians. Thus the strong claim—no Jesus, no God; no church, no Jesus.

That claim is the heart of the next three sermons on the Trinity, the crucifixion, and sacrifice. Some may think these three sermons the most theologically basic. There is no question that they deal with matters at the heart of the Christian faith, but I think that true of all the sermons in this book.[20] However, the sermons in "Saying" are meant to challenge widespread misunderstandings and outright mistakes many Christians have today about Trinity, crucifixion, and sacrifice. "The End of Sacrifice" I think particularly important, drawing as it does on my understanding of the Trinity to challenge accounts of salvation that isolate the atonement from its Christological and ecclesial context.[21]

The sermons in "Living" deal with the so-called "brass tacks" of life— that is, when all is said and done, we are born, we must learn to live with one another, and we die. Each of these sermons try to show the difference being Christian makes for how we deal with these basic realities. In particular I think the reader may be surprised how these sermons are at once "conservative" and "radical." For example I refuse to "explain" what Jesus must have "really" meant by suggesting "the poor you will always have with you" because I think attempts to explain what he really must have meant fail to remember that the poor we will always have with us is Jesus. The Christological center of the sermon "Blinded by the Light" hopefully illumines what I suspect some will find to be a startling refusal to make Christian discipleship just another way to underwrite widespread presumptions in our time about what it means to be "ethical."

The sermons on death and baptism are obviously interrelated. But I have chosen to put the baptism sermons and the sermon for a marriage and ordination in a separate section, not only because baptism is the necessary action to make intelligible marriage and ordination, but because these sermons make unavoidable the liturgical action that is the background for the whole book. That most of these sermons end directing attention to the Eucharist should also make clear my conviction that Word and sacrament cannot be separated.

The short essays in the Appendix are included because I think they help make clear what I am trying to do by collecting these sermons in a single volume. "Making the Familiar Strange" is what the sermons try to do. Indeed I hope the reader notices how often in the sermons I use or call attention to the language of collects, prayers, and responses in the liturgy. I do so because I want to remind us that what I may suggest in the sermon may sound strange, but it is no less strange than what we say every Sunday when we, for example, say "Christ has died, Christ is risen, Christ will come again."

"Preaching Repentance in a Time of War" makes explicit what I hope is apparent from the first to the last of these sermons, that is, that I believe that Christ has brought an end to war.[22] I am, however, much more direct in my critique of the American "war on terrorism" in this essay than I am in any of the sermons in this book[23] Yet it is my hope that all these sermons are as anti-war as this essay.

Finally, I have included "Connecting Some of the Dots, or An Attempt to Understand Myself" because I thought it might be helpful for those who are not acquainted with "my work." I hate the phrase "my work" because it sounds so pretentious, but I cannot deny that there is a mass of writing out there for which I must take responsibility. I do not expect readers to be familiar with all or even some of what I have done. So I thought it useful to include this short piece in the hope it might help some understand better why the sermon is one of the primary places I think the work of theology should be done.

I have also included this essay because in it I make the claim, a claim I hope is true, that I am first and foremost a theologian. I confess one of the most frustrating aspects of the criticisms made of my work is how seldom those criticisms take seriously the way I try to do theology. Admittedly I seldom do theology "straight," but that does not mean that I am not, for example, thinking about Trinity as I try to help us face death as Christians.

One final word—please do not be afraid to laugh as you read these sermons.

Part I

SEEING

1

Believing Is Seeing

Duke Chapel
March 30, 2008

Isaiah 26:2–9, 19
1 John 5:1–6
John 20:19–31

C hristians are often tempted, particularly in this time called modern, to say more than we know. We are so tempted because we fear we do not believe what we say we believe. So we try to assure ourselves that we believe what we say we believe by convincing those who do not believe what we believe that they really believe what we believe once what we believe is properly explained. As a result we end up saying more than we know because what we believe—or better, what we do—cannot be explained but only shown. The word we have been given for such a showing is "witness."

Our penchant for explanation, however, means we are continually frustrated by the Scripture. We think if the Gospels provided more fulsome accounts, newspaper-like accounts that could be checked by reputable historians, this business of belief might make more sense.

Therefore when John tells us, "Now Jesus did many other signs in the presence of his disciples, which are not written in this book," we cannot help but think that the omission was surely a mistake. We need all the signs we can get. In particular we think we need to know more because we have been made aware that the Bible may not be reliable. We are desperate, therefore, to know "what really happened."

Signs are, of course, the heart of the Gospel of John. For example, to name just a few that John does include: Jesus turns water into wine at the wedding feast in Cana (2:1–11); he heals the son of the royal official (4:46–54); he restores sight to a man born blind (9:1–41); he raises Lazarus from the dead (11:1–44); and he is resurrected (20:1–10). For John, however, signs are not irrefutable evidence that Jesus really is who he says he is. For example, most of us think if we had been there when Jesus raised Lazarus from the dead we would have been impressed by this miracle. John, however, tells us that some who had seen what Jesus had done "believed in him, but some of them went to the Pharisees and told them what he had done" (11:45–46). Signs, it seems, are just as likely to create doubt and opposition as they are to make believers.

Two thousand years after the resurrection we, like Thomas, desire a sign to calm our doubts. For we live in a culture that has taught us to demand evidence for what we believe. We are taught not to trust what we see or hear and it is a lesson we have learned well. Accordingly, we not only do not trust what we hear from others but we do not trust what we say to ourselves. And because we do not trust ourselves, we distrust what we hear as well as what we see. Ask any lawyer if they trust eyewitness testimony. So like Thomas we want to put our finger in his nail-pierced hands and touch his wounded side. Not able to trust what we hear or what we see, we need to touch that which we fear may be an illusion.

Trust is the heart of the matter. Thus Rowan Williams, the archbishop of Canterbury, makes trust the central motif in his exploration of the Apostles' and Nicene Creeds in his book *Tokens of Trust*. Williams observes that mistrust is the result of our sense that too often we feel we are at the mercy of someone else's agenda. In particular, we do not trust God because we think God has purposes we cannot fathom. As a result, attempts to "be religious" ironically can result in efforts to avoid God by outwitting him. We think of God as "the management" who is, if possible, to be outmaneuvered. Jesus's invitation to Thomas to touch his wounds is the gesture that should forever end our presumption that we can manage God.

A week after Jesus had appeared to the disciples in the closed chamber he appears again and this time Thomas is present. Jesus greets the disciples with the now familiar declaration, "Peace be with you." Jesus had previously bestowed his peace by breathing on the disciples, but he now offers Thomas his very body: "Put your finger here and see my hands. Reach out your hand and put it in my side. Do not doubt but believe."

We should like to think Thomas touches Jesus's wounds. Artists have often depicted Thomas touching Jesus. Yet the text does not give any indication Thomas in fact touched the wounds in Jesus's hands or his side. Instead we are told he confesses, "My Lord and my God!" What an extraordinary thing for Thomas to say. If he were like us, that is, looking for evidence to confirm that Jesus had returned from the dead, you would think he might have said, "Oh! You're really back." But he says, "My Lord and my God!"

This confession is not one that can be elicited by seeing or touching, but rather one that comes through the peace bestowed by the Holy Spirit. Jesus acknowledges Thomas's faith but comments, "Have you believed because you have seen me? Blessed are those who have not seen and yet have come to believe." Thomas has seen Jesus, but his confession makes clear that he has been able to see because he now believes that this Jesus is Lord and God; that is, Jesus alone is the One who has the authority to bestow the Spirit of forgiveness.

We say that "seeing is believing," but it seems in matters having to do with God that "believing is seeing." But believing does not mean we must accept twenty-three improbable propositions before breakfast. Rather, believing means being made participants in a way of life unintelligible if Jesus is not our Lord and our God. To so live is not to try to make the world conform to our wishes and fantasies, but rather to see truthfully the way the world is. But we do not see the way the world is

29

just by looking. We must be transformed, we must be freed from our ill-formed desires, if we are to see that this is God's Son and declare: here is the Creator and Redeemer; he has come not to condemn the world, but rather he has come that we might see the world through the eyes of its Creator and so be saved through him.

This may help us understand why John does not report on the "many other signs" Jesus did in the presence of his disciples. John does not tell us more because he thinks he has given us all we need in order to believe that Jesus is the Messiah, the Son of God, and that in so believing we may have life in his name. For it turns out that the Gospels are not information about which we get to make up our minds. Rather, as we are told in the sixth of Anglicanism's *Thirty-Nine Articles of Religion*, "Holy Scripture containeth all things necessary to salvation: so that whatsoever is not read therein, nor may be proved thereby, is not to be required of any man, that it should be believed as an article of the Faith, or be thought requisite or necessary to salvation." We are not asked to believe that the Scripture is without error, but rather that the Scripture provides everything necessary for our salvation.

Ironically, Christians who are determined to maintain that the Scripture is without error, as well as Christians who think we need more historical evidence in order to accept that Jesus is who he says, replicate in a modern form the ancient heresy of Gnosticism. They want Jesus to be a knowledge they can accept or reject, but they do not want their lives transformed by having to acknowledge "my Lord and my God!" They want to be able to understand Jesus in terms set by the world, but John, as do all the Gospels, refuses to give us more than we need for our salvation. For to confess "my Lord and my God" is, as philosophers like to say, a language-transforming proposal, requiring that we be transformed in the light of Jesus's crucifixion and resurrection.

For our salvation is not knowledge about which we get to make up our minds. Our salvation is flesh, crucified and resurrected flesh, wounded flesh. Jean Vanier, the founder of L'Arche, where those who are not mentally disabled learn to live with those who are, observes in his *Commentary on the Gospel of John* that

we can contemplate the risen body of Jesus,
a body that reveals the wounds inflicted upon him. . . .
These wounds are there for all ages and time,
to reveal the humble and forgiving love of Jesus
who accepted to go to the utter end of love.
The risen Jesus does not appear as the powerful one,
but as the wounded and forgiving one.

These wounds become his glory.
From the wound in his side flowed the waters that vivify
and heal us.
Through his wounds we are healed.
Jesus invites each one of us, through Thomas,
to touch not only his wounds,
but the wounds in others and in ourselves,
wounds that can make us hate others and ourselves
and can be a sign of separation and division.
These wounds will be transformed into a sign of forgiveness
through the love of Jesus
and will bring people together in love.
These wounds reveal that we need each other.
These wounds become the place of mutual compassion,
of indwelling
and of thanksgiving.

We, too, will show our wounds
when we are with him in the kingdom,
revealing our brokenness
and the healing power of Jesus.

Jesus is the wound of the Father's love, which we share through the gift of the Spirit. Let us confess we would prefer a savior not wounded, not wanting our own wounds exposed. Then let us recognize that such wounds are necessary for seeing the world and ourselves truthfully. And so, to be so wounded by the Spirit is what it means to be blessed, to be among those who have not seen but who have come to believe. Indeed, the Church is constituted by those who have come to believe what we have not seen by trusting in what we have been told. Through the work of the Spirit, our wounds of mistrust have been healed and are continually mended by the ongoing renewal of trust reenacted through the bread and wine, which is the body and blood of our Savior.

We are able to see this miracle not because we've acquired more knowledge than others, but because we have been made participants in the kingdom of forgiveness, a kingdom of peace, making possible a life otherwise unimaginable. Accordingly Jesus invites us not only to touch his wounds, but to come and taste the goodness of his life. What extraordinary good news—we can trust what we hear, we can trust what we see, we can trust what we touch, we can trust what we taste—because we have been given all we need to confess "my Lord and my God!" Alleluia, he is risen indeed. Alleluia.

2

Blinded by the Light

A Sermon for the Church of the Holy Family
Fourth Sunday of Lent
March 2, 2008

1 Samuel 16:1–13
Psalm 23
Ephesians 5:8–14
John 9:1–41

The story I learned in school, the story that has shaped the world in which you and I live, in broad outline goes like this: we are the climax; we have inherited the achievements of a succession of civilizations. From the Hebrews we learned to leave behind polytheism and most forms of religious superstition. From the Greeks we have been taught the power of reason through the development of philosophy and the beginnings of science. These achievements were given new power by Christians who, drawing on both Jewish and Greek sources, transformed the Roman Empire to create what we now call Western civilization.

Unfortunately this story of progress was sidetracked for centuries by what is called the Middle Ages or, more pejoratively, the Dark Ages. During those dark times the human spirit was suppressed by an authoritarian religious regime that legitimated repressive forms of political rule. But with the Reformation the freedom essential to human development was rediscovered. That freedom found political expression through the American and French revolutions.

The pivotal moment in these developments is called the Enlightenment. This name marks the time, a time beginning with the eighteenth century, we learned, in the words of Kant's famous slogan, to "have the courage to use our own reason." Through the use of reason, moreover, we have found the means to free ourselves from the limits of nature, disease, and death.

America is the name that sums up these developments. We are the society and the politics, a democratic politics, which exemplifies this birth of human freedom, this movement from darkness to light. We are, as it says on the dollar, *novus ordo seclorum*, the New Order of Ages. As Americans we are aware that we have yet to be all we should like to be, but we are confident that if any people deserve the description "enlightened," it is the American people.

Our enlightened status is only confirmed because we understand that the story I have told is far too simple. For example, we know that not everything about the Dark Ages was dark. We know the Greeks as well as many of those identified with the Enlightenment had slaves. Yet our ability to identify the wrongs of the past assumes the broad outline of the story I have told is true. We simply cannot imagine living in any other world.

That is certainly true for me. I may be a theologian but I am an academic. That means I am a servant of that great institution of the Enlightenment, the university. Even though I am a theologian many assume my task is to show that what we believe as Christians is not incompatible with the story of the Enlightenment. For example, I know the power the story I have told has on my life by my response to the question the disciples ask: "Rabbi, who sinned, this man or his parents, that he was born blind?" I am a representative of the Enlightenment.

I know the answer to that question: no one sinned—he was just born blind.

I should like to think that Jesus anticipates my enlightened response to his disciples' question because he refuses to accept the premise that this man's blindness had anything to do with sin. But unfortunately he rejects that premise for reasons that are even more offensive to my enlightened sensibilities than the suggestion that this man's blindness might be due to sin. Jesus says that this man was born blind so that God's work might be revealed in him. I am embarrassed by the suggestion that anyone was born blind, reduced to begging, in order that Jesus might show he had the power to heal. It is all well and good for Jesus to claim that he is "the light of the world," but he could have said that without this man's blindness.

That I have this response, as I suspect many of you do as well, is an indication of the hold the story with which I began has on our lives. Does this mean we should rethink our assumption that we stand in the light? Could it possibly be the case that I am, that we are, blinded by the light? Could it be that the story I have told, the story I suspect grips you as it grips me, makes it impossible for us to see Jesus? How could that be? Are we not the most enlightened people the world has ever known? Surely if anyone can see Jesus it must be people like us. I suspect, like Samuel trying to choose the king from Jesse's sons, we assume we would know what a king or savior should look like. But we do not see kings, saviors, or the world just by looking. Rather, Jesus claims we learn what it might mean for the world to be saved by learning to see him.

Learning to see Jesus entails a training that challenges our presumption that we are already in the light. The man born blind is able to see Jesus because he had the advantage of being born blind. We fail to see Jesus because we have the disadvantage of being enlightened. It turns out, moreover, that we cannot will our way out of our enlightened darkness. Rather, we must be confronted by a light so brilliant that we are able to see the darkness our pride mistakes as light. An extraordinary claim, but what do you expect? We are Christians after all. We worship a crucified God—that takes some getting used to.

We were told at the very beginning of the Gospel of John that the light would shine in the darkness but the darkness would not overcome it. Now we begin to understand that the darkness does not know itself as darkness until it encounters the light. This is why we are loath to give up the darkness, because we cannot imagine what it would mean to live in the light of Christ. Ask yourself, for example, what might it mean to see those born blind, to see those desperately ill, to see those in inexplicable suffering in the light of Christ? We must submit to being overcome by Christ's light in order to see the darkness that presently blinds us.

Everyone in our Scripture for today finds it hard to see rightly what Jesus has done. After the blind man comes back from washing his eyes in the pool of Siloam, many of his neighbors are unsure if he is the same beggar they knew had been blind from birth. He insists he is the same man, but the account he gives for how his eyes were opened only seems to make it more difficult to confirm that he is the same one who was born blind. Moreover, he is not of much help because he is not even sure who healed him or where the one who restored his sight may be. He may be able to see, but he remains in the dark. Healed of his blindness, he will have to undergo training if he is to see Jesus.

The training begins by his attempt to respond to the Pharisees' questions about how he had received his sight, as well as how it could be that he had been healed on the Sabbath. The man born blind resorts to the most readily available theological theory that might explain who it is that has healed him: "He is a prophet." But the Pharisees have an equally plausible response: Jesus cannot be a prophet. Prophets are from God. They do God's will. But Jesus, if, in fact, he healed the blind man, healed him on the Sabbath. So he cannot be a prophet.

Some, who seem to have a more empirical bent, doubt if the man was ever blind. They confront his parents with the not-so-subtle suggestion that they may have lied about their son's blindness. His parents stubbornly maintain he was born blind but refuse to take sides about how or who opened his eyes. Because his parents fear they will lose their good standing in the synagogue, much like Eve they shift responsibility elsewhere, in this case to their son: "He is of age, ask him."

The man born blind is called a second time before the sagacious class of his day. They demand that he acknowledge that Jesus must be a sinner. The man whose sight has been restored is beginning to learn. He states what he knows. It is not for him to say whether Jesus is or is not a sinner. What he knows, however, is that he was blind but now he sees. His accusers press the issue. They want to know how his sight was restored. They demand an explanation. The man born blind recognizes he has nothing to lose. He even resorts to irony, asking if those who doubt he has been healed want to hear the story again in order that they might become a disciple of Jesus.

Irony, however, is seldom a weapon that persuades an adversary, particularly an adversary who is more powerful, because their power derives from the presumption that they represent what "everyone knows." So the man born blind is reviled by those who claim to possess true knowledge, the knowledge that comes from Moses, and everyone knows God spoke to Moses. The argumentative skills of the man born blind, however, are increasing. He counters their argument about Moses by pointing out that God does not listen to sinners but rather to those who worship and obey God's will. Then in an extraordinary theological move he observes that since the world began no one born blind has had their eyes opened. That his eyes have been opened must, therefore, indicate that the one who healed him is from God. Indeed it may be that Jesus not only is from God, but shares in God's very life. Such a suggestion is too much for those who think they have the knowledge of Moses. They have had enough. They resort to the first mode of explanation: "You who were born in sin are trying to teach us?" They throw him out of the synagogue.

The man born blind still does not know where Jesus may be, but Jesus, hearing of his excommunication, seeks him out. Jesus recognizes that the man he has healed has now undergone the training necessary to recognize who he is. So he asks him: "Do you believe in the Son of Man?" The formerly blind man is ready to believe, but he is not sure who the Son of Man may be. Jesus's response is telling: "You have seen him." In saying this Jesus is affirming what the blind man has otherwise not been given permission to acknowledge, namely, that Jesus is from

God. Jesus, the Son of Man, now stands before the man born blind. The man not only says, "Lord, I believe," but we are told that he worshiped Jesus. The blind man is a good Jew. As such, he can only worship God. This man, this blind man, has finally learned to see Jesus.

Jesus then makes clear what has been clear from the beginning of this extraordinary episode—he has come into the world that those who do not see may see and those who do see may become blind. Some of the Pharisees hearing this ask rhetorically if Jesus meant to suggest they might be blind. Jesus responds that because they think they see, because they assume they are already in the light, they remain blinded by the light.

Given the alternatives, if we had to identify with anyone in this narrative, most of us, I suspect, would choose to be the man born blind. But remember our reaction to Jesus's statement that this man had been born blind in order that God's work might be revealed in him. Even after we have been healed by Jesus I suspect most of us could not help but feel a bit misused. Which is another reminder of what a radical transformation is required, particularly for those of us who pride ourselves on being enlightened, if we are to see Jesus as the very Son of Man and Son of God.

Paul writes to the Ephesians, reminding them that they once were in darkness, but now they are "in the Lord," which means, Paul says, "you are the light." As children of the light we are to bear fruit because the light is found in all that is good, right, and true. Paul then urges the Ephesians to try to find what is pleasing to the Lord by doing nothing in secret that cannot be made visible to the whole church. For it is through such a process, a process that can never be finished, that we discover what is pleasing to the Lord for our time and place.

Such a process, such a training, is required if we are to discern what is good, what is right, what is true about our story of enlightenment. I am not suggesting that everything about that story is evil, wrong, or false. Rather, I am suggesting that, as people shaped by that story, we are going to need all the help we can get if we are to discern, as Paul argues we must, what it means to live in the light of Jesus and to be that light for the world. The great challenge is not how we can fit Jesus into the story of the Enlightenment, but how the story of the Enlightenment is to be judged by Jesus.

For let us confess that our story, the self-congratulatory story of our enlightened status, can make it difficult for us to see and worship Jesus. We want Jesus to confirm what we have learned from a world that cannot believe that the Father would redeem the world through the gift of the Son. The world in which we live would tempt us to believe that our prayers for healing are only meant to show that we care for one another. The world in which we live would have us describe this bread and wine as symbols but not the reality of the body and blood of Jesus.

If we are to be the light of Christ we must have our lives illumined by those Christians who have other stories to tell than the story we tell of our enlightened status as Americans. We will only learn to see Jesus if we learn to listen to how their vision has been shaped by their speech. To undergo such training will be painful and will require great patience. It may be as hard and demanding as trying to understand one of Bishop Ochola's[1] stories or what it means for Haitian Christians to engage in the slow, hard work of building a school.

I do not know how our learning to listen to the stories of Christians in different times and places will change our story. I do not know what it will mean for the kind of education we give our children. I do not know what it will mean for how we understand ourselves as Americans. I do not know what it will mean for how we negotiate a world in which the means we use to gain control of fate and death make us ever more fated by our own creations. But I do know we will only begin to know how to answer such questions if, like the man born blind, we learn to see and worship Jesus.

3

So Much Depends

Sermon for the Ekklesia Project
Annual Meeting
July 16, 2007

Matthew 13:24–32

so much depends
upon
a red wheel
barrow
glazed with rain
water
beside the white
chickens

> William Carlos
> Williams

S o much depends upon the poet whose words make possible our seeing what otherwise could not be seen. We can only act in a world we can see, but we cannot see just by looking. Rather we can only see what we can say. So it seems the limit of our language is the limit of our world. Yet we know from our language that the world exists independently of our wills, so it cannot be just "our world." We must wrestle with our language, therefore, if we are to avoid subjecting the world to our desire that the world be no more than "our world." Poetry is the struggle some make with language to stretch our speech, and therefore ourselves, so that we might better say "this is how things are."

So much depends on the Word who in the beginning was with God. "In the beginning was the deed" and the Word that was the deed created language. That the Word created language means language cannot but witness to the deed of its own creation. But "words are also deeds" capable of testifying to the wonder of their existence. Because words are also deeds we are tempted to forget that they too are created. Yet the Word who was in the beginning with God became one of us, creating and redeeming our world by stretching our words. A new creation, a new world, was begun. So there is now another world, but it is the same one as this world. A new world created within the old world, however, cannot help but be a world in crisis.

Jesus taught in parables to help us see the crisis that otherwise cannot be seen. The parables are not poems, but like poems the parables invite comparisons—"The kingdom of heaven may be compared . . ."—and comparisons often seem poetic. Thus C. H. Dodd's definition of a parable: "At its simplest the parable is a metaphor or simile drawn from nature of common life, arresting the hearer by its vividness or strangeness, and leaving the mind in sufficient doubt about its precise application to tease it into active thought." To which one can only say, "Dear Lord, please save me from ever being tempted to define anything."

However, Dodd's characterization of a parable is helpful because it reminds us that parables, like poetry, use the everyday to help us discover the sheer givenness, the remarkable oddness, of the everyday. That a happenstance rain glazed a red wheelbarrow brightening the whiteness of chickens can be missed. But once the poet positions the words, we not only see what we have seen, but our sight is refreshed and makes visible similar contingencies otherwise missed. So Jesus in his parables uses what we know to make what we know strange.

41

At the heart of Aquinas's theological work is the presumption that all existence, that is, every single creature, is a testimony, a witness to the wisdom of God the artist. Aquinas observes that

> all creatures are compared to God as artifacts to an artist . . . Whence the whole of nature is like a certain artifact of the divine art. It is not, however, opposed to the nature of an artifact that the artist should work in a different way on his product even after he has given it its first form. Nor therefore is it against nature that God should work otherwise in natural things than as the customary course of nature operates.

And in turn this means nothing could be more natural than the incarnation. Very God and very man is the parable of the Second person of the Trinity. Accordingly the parables testify to the very character of creation. Parables are the grammatical form commensurate to the ontological character of our existence. Thus John Howard Yoder, the great metaphysician of contemporary theology, claims

> when God chose Jesus as the way to come into the world, when Jesus chose disciples as a way to make his message mobile, and when the disciples chose the "gospel" as preferred literary form of witness, each meant the choice of the story of the holy one as the dominant prototype not only of communicating, but of being good news. Jesus' parables, like his presenting himself as model, did not represent a mere pedagogical choice of "storytelling" as a more understandable way to communicate to illiterate crowds; the story is rather in the order of being and in the order of knowing the more fundamental mode of reality.

Jesus is the parable of the Father's love given to transform us so that we might be drawn into the new creation called the kingdom of God. So we should not be surprised that artists who make the known unknown and the unknown known through words and images find themselves drawn to the sheer contingency of the incarnation. For it turns out that learning to see the contingent, indeed learning to see the beauty of the contingent, is not easy, desiring as we do not to have the contingency of our lives revealed. Yet artists know, or at least they should know, that they can only imitate the true artist, because only

God can create the singulars which constitute the world. So the artist must undergo training, a willing submission to a singular, which is not unlike learning to be a disciple.

The crowd gathers around Jesus and he teaches them using parables, but he tells his disciples he does this so that "seeing they do not perceive, and hearing they do not listen, nor do they understand." By his use of parables Jesus changes the very meaning of "understanding." Seeking to understand the parables requires that we be drawn into the new creation Jesus has inaugurated. To be drawn into the new creation means we must be willing to follow him to Jerusalem where he will be crucified—the climax of the crisis began with his conception.

The parables must, therefore, like the whole Scripture, be read Christologically. We only know what they mean, indeed we only know why it may not be very helpful to ask what they mean, in light of the crucifixion and resurrection of Jesus. The familiar character of the parables is why they are so deceptive and why we so often get them wrong. They deal with matters that are so everyday—seeds sown on rocky ground, fields of weeds and wheat, mustard seeds, hidden treasures, pearls, and fishing with nets. This seems like everyday stuff, but it is because the parables are clothed in everyday words that we are tempted to employ them as if no crisis exists. The parables, in contrast to the Sermon on the Mount, seem to offer the kind of wisdom we can use to help us— and we assume the parables are about us—to negotiate life. As you grow older, for example, you learn that what you thought was a weed was actually wheat, so do not be in a hurry to make judgments you will later regret. Live and let live.

Reinhold Niebuhr thought he understood what the parable of the weeds and wheat meant. According to Niebuhr the parable teaches us that in the world as we know it there will be times when Christians will have to kill, but when we do so we should do it with humility. For in this time—that is, the time judged by the cross that stands as the edge of history—we must recognize that it is as true of those who are Christians as those who are not that our loves are infected by love of self. It is, therefore, impossible for us—that is, those who call ourselves Christians—to distinguish the weeds from the wheat.

There is much to be said for Niebuhr-like readings, but such readings ignore the apocalyptic character of the parables, that is, that the parables presume the new creation in the old. Thus Jesus explains the parable to his disciples making clear that the good seeds are those sown by the Son of Man and the weeds are those sown by the devil. At the end of the age the Son of Man will send his angels and they will collect out of his kingdom all the evildoers and throw them into a furnace of fire where there will be weeping and gnashing of teeth. Surely this dramatic language is sufficient to make us sympathetic with Niebuhr's interpretation of the parable as an account of the ambiguity of all our attempts at justice. But the apocalyptic language is a reminder that the new creation has begun, the Son of Man has come, his name is Jesus, and his way in the world is the way of nonviolence.

Of course I am preaching to the choir. We are the Ekklesia Project.[1] We are those, as our declaration states, who believe that "to 'be the Church' is to declare that our allegiance to the God of Jesus Christ always takes priority over other structures that compete for our attention during every hour of every day of our lives. . . . We are 'called out' from the world, as suggested by the original Greek word for church: ekklesia. We understand this 'calling out' to be the work of the Holy Spirit, who redeems the lives of believers not as isolated individuals, but as members of an alternative community—a resource of resistance to the social and political structures of the age."

In short, we cannot help but think we are the wheat, we are the mustard seed, and we are damned tired of the waiting. We have no use for the accommodated church. We have no use for Christians who "conform their lives to partisan ideologies and identities, or to the routines of a consumer culture." But if we are so radical, if we are the apocalyptic mustard seeds, what in the hell are we doing here engaging in the play world of academics by pretending we enjoy having our imaginations enriched by reading poetry? Are we what God's new creation looks like? Surely we look too normal to be God's people.

But let us hope that, without too much self-deception, we may learn to see our normality as a witness to the kingdom to which the parables point. In his extraordinary presidential address in 1988 to the Society of Christian Ethics, "To Serve God and Rule the World," John Howard Yoder suggested that to see history doxologically, which I take it the parables are meant to do, means Christians must avoid utopian fantasies. Accordingly, Yoder suggests that "'to rule the world' in fellowship with the living Lamb will sometimes mean humbly building a grassroots culture, with Jeremiah. Sometimes (as with Joseph and Daniel) it will mean helping the pagan king solve one problem at a time. Sometimes it will mean disobeying the King's imperative of idolatry, refusing to be bamboozled by the claims made for the Emperor's new robe or his fiery furnace." In short, to be God's parable for the world means we cannot pretend to be more than we are.

If we are to avoid fantasy and pretense, however, much will depend on how we have learned to allow the Word, Jesus Christ, to shape our words. So much will depend on our being made into Christ's body by the words that speak us. So much will depend on those who have patiently attended to the hard work of word care that we might see the bright beauty of God's kingdom in the blood washed white of the martyrs' robes. And so much will depend on our seeing in and with one another that

> the just man justices;
> Keeps grace: that keeps all his goings graces;
> Acts in God's eye what in God's eye he is—
> Christ. For Christ plays in ten thousand places,
> Lovely in limbs, and lovely in eyes not his,
> To the Father through the features of men's faces.

So may we, even here, learn to help one another see.

4

Witness

A Sermon for the Divinity School at Duke University
Feast of Saint Luke
October 18, 2007

Ecclesiasticus 38:1–4, 6–10, 12–14
Psalm 147:1–7
2 Timothy 4:5–13
Luke 4:14–21

I moved to South Bend, Indiana, in 1970 to teach at the University of Notre Dame. In 1970 South Bend still had a downtown with department stores. One of those stores was named Gilberts. Gilberts was a fashionable men's store that specialized in selling tailored suits to well-off gentlemen. One of the ways Gilberts emphasized its elite status was to suggest the way you learned of Gilberts's excellence was "One man tells another." The only problem with that claim is that the way Gilberts used to get the message out that "One man tells another" was by advertising on television. In fairness it must be said that Gilberts had to resort to commercials in an effort to compete with men's clothing stores in the malls that were beginning to surround South Bend.

In the fourteen years I lived in South Bend I learned to love the Midwest and its people. Yet I also learned that those down-to-earth people who live in the Midwest are not long on irony. No one in South Bend seemed amused by the claim that the way the word about Gilberts got around, that is, that one man had to tell another, was known primarily through commercials on television. Gilberts, like the other department stores in downtown South Bend, eventually had to close—the malls won. That's capitalism.

The gospel *is* known by one person telling another. One person must tell another because the gospel is a story. There is no truth, there is no summary of the story, that can be separated from the story itself. In particular, the gospel is the story of Jesus, the messiah of Israel, and it is a story known only because it has been told and retold through witnesses across time and space. These witnesses, moreover, actually become part of the story such that the teller and the tale become one.

Indeed the witnesses become so much a part of the story that the retelling must incorporate an account of their lives if the story is to be truthfully told. We call such people "saints" because they have endured much for the sake of the story, in line with Paul's admonition: "As for you, always be sober, endure suffering, do the work of the evangelist, carry out your ministry fully." Indeed the suffering some must endure requires that they die rather than betray the story. We call these witnesses "martyrs."

Today we celebrate the feast of a saint called Luke. We do so because Luke, under the guidance of the Spirit, thought Theophilus needed an orderly account so that he might know the truth concerning the things about which he had been instructed. "Orderly account" is Luke's way of saying "story." But does our celebration of Luke call into question my claim that the way we learn the gospel is through one person telling another? Why do you need to be a witness if you have a text? Might we presume Luke was simply using the technology of his day to make the gospel available to anyone without the necessity of a witness? If he had had television, might Luke have written a commercial for Jesus?

The answer to these questions is very simple—the reason Luke's Gospel does not replace the necessity of witnesses is because of the way Luke tells Theophilus the story. For what we learn from Luke is the necessity of witness through the work of the Spirit. Luke tells us the story of Jesus, but to tell that story he must introduce another character, the Holy Spirit. This character appears at Jesus's baptism in the person of the Spirit, who descends upon Jesus in a bodily form like a dove. Full of the Holy Spirit, Jesus is led into the wilderness to face the temptations of the devil—temptations designed to have Jesus resort to television-like shortcuts for the realization of the Kingdom.

The work of the Spirit in Luke means there is no way we can avoid the necessity of witnesses. Yet if that is the case, how are we to account for the peculiar absences of the Holy Spirit in recent theology? An absence that Gene Rogers explores in his book *After the Spirit* by asking: is there anything the Spirit can do that the Son cannot do better? He answers: there is something the Spirit does that the Son needs; the Spirit's work is to come to rest. So the Spirit rests on the Son signifying not only their eternal union but also their union in the temporal order. As the Orthodox theologian Dmitri Staniloae puts it, "The presence of Christ is always marked by the Spirit resting upon him, and the presence of the Spirit means the presence of Christ is upon whom he rests."

We should, therefore, not be surprised that Jesus, having bested the devil in the wilderness and being "filled with the power of the Spirit," returns to Galilee to teach in the synagogues. Perhaps even more daunting than facing the devil is Jesus's return home to Nazareth where, in the synagogue, he reads from the scroll given him these words from the sixty-first chapter of Isaiah: "The Spirit of the Lord is upon me." And after reading, Jesus announces, "Today this Scripture has been fulfilled in your hearing." The Spirit has named the One who from the beginning was to be the Spirit's rest, and those in attendance have been made witnesses.

That the Spirit has come to rest on Jesus through his reading of Isaiah confirms Rogers's contention that the "Spirit is a Person with an affinity for material things. The Spirit characteristically befriends the body" and, in particular, the body of Jesus. This being the case, it is not insignificant that the one telling us this story is a physician himself.

We are instructed by Ecclesiasticus to give thanks for physicians who have been given the gift of healing from the Most High. For "the Lord created medicines out of the earth, and the sensible will not despise them." So physicians learn to heal by touch, by using their hands to learn the stories the body has to tell—one body at a time. Luke, therefore, uses his skill as a physician to tell the story of the bodily work of the Spirit. Listen again, therefore, to the collect for today:

> Almighty God, who inspired your servant Luke the physician to set forth in the Gospel the love and healing power of your Son: Graciously continue in your Church this love and power to heal, to the praise and glory of your Name: through Jesus Christ our Lord, who lives and reigns with you, in the unity of the Holy Spirit, one God, now and forever. Amen.

As a physician Luke is keenly aware of the bodily character of the Spirit's work through the Incarnate Son. But Luke is equally concerned with the implications of the Spirit's work through the Body of Christ, which is the continuation of the Spirit's work in the Son. It is the same Spirit, as Luke tells the story, which comes to rest on the church, making us the body of Christ.

It is worth noting that Luke's story of Jesus does not end with Jesus's ascension, because the Spirit has further work to do that the ascension not only makes possible but necessary. The church is that further work. But that work turns out to be a particular action in which, through the power of the Holy Spirit, one person tells another person the story of Jesus. That is why the Gospel of Luke is not a commercial. It is not a commercial because Luke makes us, the church, witnesses and therefore constitutive of the story.

There are no short cuts for the spreading of the Gospel. Luke, the great chronicler of the Spirit, makes it unmistakably clear that without Jesus we know not what we say when we say "God," but without the church we do not know Jesus. Jesus is known through the bodily witness of the Spirit who comes to rest by wildly creating a people across time and space. Indeed, Luke has so much to say about this people that he writes Acts. Under the inspiration of the Spirit Luke provides us with an "orderly account" of the work of the Spirit, in which the witness of

49

Luke is itself taken up into the story. So when we celebrate the Feast of Saint Luke we do so by acknowledging that the same Spirit that guides and constitutes Luke's witness also makes it possible for us to participate as witnesses to that same story. Saints are remarkable, but without a remarkable community they cannot be acknowledged. Interestingly enough, Luke is the saint whose story of the work of the Spirit makes clear the inseparability of church and saints.

Today's collect rightly reminds us that Luke's Gospel, Luke's bodily gospel of healing, is also the gospel of love. For to be healed is to have our bodies storied by the Spirit who teaches us how to love and be loved as the Father loves the Son and the Son loves the Father. In the words of Eugene Rogers, for Luke the Holy Spirit is

> witness to that love in particular circumstances—those of the solidarity of the Son with human beings, even unto death. She is the witness to a marriage feast, that of God and humanity, which turns out, with the death of Jesus, to be a deathbed wedding. In those circumstances she keeps faith with the office of a witness to a wedding: she plays its guarantor; she works to hold it together. The Spirit witnesses to the love between the Father and the Son, and it is therefore her characteristic but unexacted gift to the Son that she creates witnesses to that love also among human beings.

The love that creates us to be witnesses, to be present bodily to one another, is here present in the body and blood of Jesus. The Spirit comes to rest on this bread and wine making them the body and blood of Christ. That the Spirit does so makes us Christ's body for the world. Here we are made witnesses in time, witnesses who have been given the time to tell one person at a time the good news that all time has been redeemed. Only such a people can be good news for the poor, sight for the blind, hope for the captives and oppressed. Today, in the reading of the gospel, the Scripture is fulfilled.

Part II

SAYING

5

The Glory of the Trinity

A Sermon for the Church of the Holy Family
June 3, 2007

Isaiah 6:1–8
Revelation 4:1–11
John 16:5–15
Psalm 29

Holy, holy, holy is the Lord of hosts;
The whole earth is full of his glory.

P raise of the Holy One of Israel made Israel a people. That is why the Psalms are the heart of Israel's life. Israel did not begin with an idea of God, what we might identify today as monotheism, but rather she learned to worship the One who alone is worthy of worship. Through praise Israel discovered a firm line must be drawn between God and creatures. Worship signaled what theologians, Jewish and Christian, would later identify as "the distinction," that is, that God is God and we are not. It is "the distinction" because all other distinctions depend on it. "The distinction" means no matter how exalted any creatures may appear, including the gods addressed in our Psalm, they remain creatures.

It is not surprising, therefore, that Isaiah is overwhelmed by his vision of the Holy One of Israel. The seraphs, which like Isaiah are creatures, covered their faces in the presence of the Lord. Isaiah, a mere human, is faced by the glory of God—a glory that was believed to be fatal should any mortal encounter it directly. That glory, in the words of our Psalm, is the beauty of holiness, a beauty that illumines all that God has created. Thus, after the seraphs sing, "Holy, holy, holy is the Lord of hosts," they also celebrate that "the whole earth is full of God's glory." Instructed by the psalm, we follow the seraphs' example and join the music of creation singing, "The voice of the Lord is upon the waters." The glory of the Holy One of Israel, the Creator of all that is, is here present in the beauty of creation.

Praise is not an "add on" to knowledge gained through other ways of knowing. Rather, praise is the condition necessary for our being able to see ourselves and all that is as God's creation, that is, to see the contingent and beautiful intricacy of the world as manifestation of God's glory. Praise is God's good gift through which we participate with all creation in the joyful recognition that all that is was created to worship God. Through praise we learn to acknowledge that God is always beyond whatever we imagine to be "the beyond." Yet the same God abides in absolute intimacy with creation. God's beauty, God's terrifying beauty of holiness, at once embraces and exceeds all that is.

Israel, the people who God called from the nations to be a holy people, time and time again was tempted to turn the gift of praise into a possession. The description Israel used to name her sinful desire to live in denial of "the distinction" was "idolatry." To be sure, idolatry took the form of worshiping gods other than the Holy One of Israel, but Israel knew well that the subtlest form of idolatry was to make God a thing at our disposal. Yet God refused to be idolized and sent his prophets, prophets like Isaiah, a man of unclean lips among people of unclean lips, so that Israel might become a people of truth.

Like Isaiah, John the Seer stands before the throne of God. The throne is surrounded by creatures—magnificent and strange creatures—who exist only to reflect God's glory. Again they sing:

> Holy, holy, holy
> the Lord God the Almighty,
> > who was and is and is to
> > come.
> You are worthy, our Lord and God,
> > to receive glory and honor and power,
> for you created all things,
> > and by your will they existed and were created.

John's vision, like that of Isaiah's, makes clear that the early church understood "the distinction" between God and creation. Christians worship Israel's God. Christians, like Israel, learn our faith by singing the Psalms. Christians, no less than Israel, must avoid idolatry. Christians, no less than Israel, are who we are through the adoration of the Source of all life.

Yet the Seer of Revelation also sees what Isaiah had not seen. He sees a Lamb take a scroll from the One seated on the throne. When the Lamb takes the scroll, immediately the four living creatures and the twenty-four elders who had surrounded the throne fall down before the Lamb and sing this new song (Rev. 5:9–13):

> You are worthy to take the scroll
> and to open its seal,
> for you were slaughtered and by
> > your blood you ransomed for God
> saints from every tribe and
> > language and people
> > and nation;
> you have made them to be a kingdom
> > and priests serving our God,
> and they will reign on earth.

The angels surrounding the throne are joined by thousands of living creatures and elders singing:

Worthy is the Lamb that was
    slaughtered
to receive power and wealth and
    wisdom and might
and honor and glory and blessing!
To the one seated on the throne
    and to the Lamb
be blessing and honor and glory
    and might
forever and ever!

Christians, who have learned from Israel "the distinction" between God and creation, the distinction that is at the heart of what we do when we worship God, praise and worship Jesus. We worship Jesus, the very one who took on our flesh, who for our sake became a creature. How can this be if we are to honor "the distinction"? The answer is the mystery we identify as the holy Trinity.

In our gospel for today Jesus tells us that he is going to the Father, to the One who sent him, so that the Advocate can come. Jesus will be raised from the dead never to die again, but it is not the resurrection about which he speaks when he tells his disciples he must "go away." Rather his going away means he will ascend to the right hand of the Father. His ascension makes the vision reported by John possible. Because of his ascension we not only can worship him but we necessarily do so. We do so under the direction of the Spirit, whose task it is to witness to Jesus by drawing us into the very life of the One who has come that the world might see the beauty of his holiness.

Trinity is not the result of abstract metaphysical speculation about how one god can be three. Trinity is not an explanation. Rather, Trinity names the mystery that is the very life of God. God, therefore, is the name we use to indicate the love that constitutes the relation Jesus and his Father share through the Spirit. God is the description we use to celebrate the Father's sending of the Son and the Son's doing the Father's will so that the work of the Spirit might be fulfilled by judging the world in truth.

So the assumption, a widespread assumption I fear, that Trinity is a further elaboration of a prior idea of god—again, an idea that might be called monotheism—is simply idolatry. It is to make God a thing rather than the One Isaiah and John praise as the Holy One of Israel. Such a view assumes we must have some idea of god; something must have started it all, which we then try to connect with Jesus. Thus the presumption that Father is the name we give god as Creator, Jesus names god as Savior, and Spirit—well, we are not sure what the Spirit may do other than validate some experience we associate with being religious. We then wonder if each of these names can be a name for the same God.

Like Israel, however, Christians do not begin with an abstract idea of god. Rather, like Israel, we begin:

> Holy, holy, holy is the Lord of hosts;
> The whole earth is full of his glory.

That is why the heart of our confession that God is Triune is the church's insistence that the God we worship, the Father, Son, and Holy Spirit, is Israel's God. Like Israel we have learned we cannot know who God is in himself. Like Israel we have learned that our language is never adequate to say who God is. In the words of Thomas Aquinas, "we are joined to God as to One Unknown."

But with Israel we believe the whole earth is full of the glory of God. We believe, moreover, that glory found its decisive home in the life, death, resurrection, and ascension of Jesus Christ. The mystery of the Trinity is the indivisible work of the Spirit who with the Father and the Son creates; the Father who redeems through the Son and Spirit; and the Son's love for the Father and the Father's love for the Son into which we are incorporated through the work of the Spirit.

Thus Augustine observes:

> For the Christian it is enough to believe that the cause of created things, whether in heaven or earth, visible or invisible, is nothing other than the goodness of the creator who is the one true God, and that there is nothing that is not either himself or from him, and that he is Trinity, that is, Father, the Son begotten of the Father and the Holy Spirit who proceeds from the same Father, and is one and the same Spirit of Father

and Son. By this Trinity, supremely, equally, and unchangeably good, all things have been created . . . and at the same time all things are very good, since in all things consists the beauty of the universe.

Yet the distinction between God and his creation remains. For only God, who is closer to us than we are to ourselves, is capable of making his home among us while remaining God. That is what Trinity names. We worship a God whose deity, as Karl Barth reminds us, is no prison in which he can exist only in and for Himself. Rather our God's freedom is to be in and for himself, but also with and for us. He is the wholly exalted One but also the One completely humble; he is the Almighty but is almighty in mercy; he is Lord but also Servant; he is our Eternal King and our Brother in time. He is all of this without in the slightest way forfeiting his deity because his deity is Trinity.

Let us confess we find a God of such unrelenting intimacy, a God who refuses to abandon his creation, difficult. We prefer a more distant god. We should not be surprised, therefore, that Jesus tells his disciples that when the Spirit of truth comes the ruler of this world will be exposed and judged. Yet Jesus also promises that the same Spirit will guide us, his people, into all truth. He does not promise that so guided we will be safe, but rather that our lives will be joined in the music of God's glory manifest in creation.

Trinity, therefore, is not a doctrine that is an "add on" to the essentials of the Christian faith. Trinity names the essentials of our faith. The good news that is the gospel is that the Father, the Son, and the Holy Spirit make possible our participation in the very life of God. The beauty that radiates from God's holiness is not a beauty that allows us to stand gawking at a safe distance. Rather God's beauty is the love that is the relation between the Father, Son, and Holy Spirit, the love that sings the miracle of creation and redemption. We are drawn into that love through the work of the Spirit. Listen to these words you will soon hear again:

We celebrate the memorial of our redemption, O Father, in this sacrifice of praise and thanksgiving. Recalling his death, resurrection, and ascension, we offer you these gifts. Sanctify them by your Holy Spirit to be for your people the Body and Blood of your Son, the holy food and drink of new and unending life in him. Sanctify us also that we may faithfully receive this holy Sacrament, and serve you in unity, constancy, and peace; and at the last day bring us with all your saints into the joy of your eternal kingdom. All this we ask through your Son Jesus Christ. By him, and with him, and in him, in the unity of the Holy Spirit all honor and glory is yours, Almighty Father, now and for ever. Amen.

According to Augustine, if we faithfully receive these gifts of Christ's body and blood we become what we receive. We become part of that great assembly constituted by praise of the One—the Father, the Son, and the Holy Spirit—who alone is worthy to be so praised. Here, through the work of the Spirit, we participate in the Father's love of the Son so that the world may see the beauty of holiness. So come, let us be overwhelmed by the glory of the Holy One of Israel who is the Trinity.

6

Was It Fitting for Jesus to Die on a Cross?

A Sermon for Duke Divinity School
on the Dedication of the Processional Cross
November 16, 2005

Philippians 2:1–11
Matthew 27:32–37

And when they had crucified him . . ." What more can be said? "And when they had crucified him . . ." Matthew does not elaborate. All we need to know is that Jesus Christ is crucified. He is nailed to a cross. That cross, moreover, is destined to become the icon of God. No matter how hard Christians strive to confirm our illusion that we can follow Jesus without suffering, we confront the stark and brutal reality of the crucifixion. We would like to believe that the crucifixion was some terrible mistake, a failure in communication, but the reality is unavoidable. He was crucified.

Why did he have to die? Why did he have to die on a cross? The latter question seems easily answered. He had to die on a cross because that is the way the Romans executed those they regarded as a threat to their power. Hang them high so that all could see what happens when you challenge Rome. But that answer is not sufficient for us to understand why he had to die on a cross. He died on a cross to reveal the very heart of God. The cross is where God's life crosses our life to create life otherwise unimaginable.

Yet Aquinas observes that "it would seem that Christ ought not to have suffered on the cross." In the Old Testament, sacrifices that prefigure Christ consisted in slaying animals by cutting their throats and subsequently consuming them with fire. So, Aquinas asks, would it not have been more appropriate for Jesus, like John the Baptist, to have had his head cut off? And would it not have been even more fitting for Jesus's severed head and body to be immolated in the holocaust of an altar? Aquinas also observes that death on a cross was a death of dishonor and malediction, as we read in Deuteronomy 21:23: "'He is accursed of God that hangeth on a tree.' Therefore it does not seem fitting for Jesus to be crucified."

"On the contrary," however, Aquinas argues that it was most fitting that Christ should suffer the death on the cross. Jesus's death on the cross was suitable in order to atone for the sin of our first parent for plucking the fruit from the forbidden tree against God's command. So it was fitting for Christ to suffer by being fastened to a tree to restore what Adam had stolen. All that Adam lost by despising God's command, Aquinas explains, quoting Augustine, "Christ found on the cross." So the cross planted into the ground yet reaching to the sky at once purifies the air and cleanses the earth, an earth bloodstained by Abel's murder, by the blood that flowed from Jesus's side.

Aquinas, moreover, argues that Christ's death on the wood of the cross was prefigured by the wood that burned the sacrifices of the altar. Of course Christ's death on the cross does not perfectly match in every respect the sacrifice of the altar, but that is the way it should be, for otherwise Christ's sacrifice would be the *same as* rather than *prefigured by* the sacrifices of the altar. Instead of actual fire consuming animal flesh, the holocaust that is the cross of Christ, like the burning bush, burns with the charity that saves us without destroying us. In like manner Chrysostom suggests that Jesus had to die on the cross and not be beheaded, as was John, because his entire and indivisible body might obey death so that we might be freed of our fear of death.

Finally, Aquinas suggests the cross was fitting because the cross signifies the universal salvation of the entire world. Aquinas agrees with Gregory of Nyssa that "the shape of the cross extending out into four extremes from their central point of contact denotes the power and the providence diffused everywhere of him who hung upon it." Thus the fittingness of the cross makes possible the church's prayer:

> Lord Jesus Christ, you stretched out your arms of love on the hard wood of the cross that everyone might come within the reach of your saving embrace: So clothe us in your Spirit that we, reaching forth our hands in love, may bring those who do not know you to the knowledge and love of you; for the honor of your Name. Amen.

We, meaning those of us who think of ourselves as modern, are tempted to think Aquinas's attempt to show why Christ had to die on a cross is fanciful or, at least, forced. Yet Aquinas rightfully helps us see how the contingent character of how Christ died now determines the way things are. The cross was a necessity, but a necessity that is only revealed by the contingent character of the cross, a contingency that— like creation itself—is the very revelation of God's love.

Jesus might have been beheaded, but he was not. Think about the difference it would have made for how we see the world, how we depict our faith, if Jesus had been beheaded. Jesus died on a cross because that is the way the Romans killed their enemies, but that he so died makes it possible for us now to see that he could have died no other way. That he could have died no other way, moreover, is why we are bold to display our faith through representations like this processional cross of the crucifixion.

It was not always so. We have almost no depictions of the crucifixion on tombs or in Christian homes or places of worship through the first four centuries. We can only speculate why that may have been the case.

Perhaps under persecution Christians were not anxious to remind their enemies that their Savior had died the death of judicial torture. But more likely the faith of the early church was determined by the resurrection. The actual event of the resurrection, as Scripture makes clear, was not and could not be seen, because God cannot be seen. Yet our faith is fleshly, requiring embodiment, which means Christians rightly could not restrain their desire to "see" the resurrected Savior. So Christians made the cross our central icon, but the Jesus depicted on the cross is the resurrected and triumphant Jesus.

The Protestant empty cross may have been an appropriate protest against baroque depictions of the crucifixion that sometimes seem designed to do little more than invite us to become spectators of an unending cruelty. However, the empty cross can tempt us to think of the cross as but a symbol of God's mercy and love. It is, therefore, appropriate that at this Protestant divinity school our processional cross is not empty. The body of Jesus dominates the cross, making it impossible for us to forget that the resurrected Jesus is the crucified Jesus. On this cross his hands are pierced, but they are not nailed down. The Son has suffered and still suffers for our sins, but his suffering through the resurrection has defeated all that would stand in the way of our receiving the gift of the Father's love.

Christ on this cross remains gaunt, making it impossible for us to forget that a sacrifice of suffering has been made. Yet this cross, as any cross should be, is beautiful. Indeed that is why it is so important that Aquinas explored the "fittingness" of the cross. "Fitting" is but another word for beauty. Art is the ongoing attempt to help us discover that which is fitting, but the beauty of the fitting we can fail to see if we do not have the help of the artist. In *Grace and Necessity: Reflections on Art and Love*, Rowan Williams observes that "the artist looks for the 'necessity' in the thing being made, but this 'necessity' can only be shown when the actual artistic form somehow lets you know that the necessity is not imposed by the hand of an artistic will but uncovered as underlying the real contingency of a world that has been truthfully imagined."

Yet the artist can only "make." God alone is the artist capable of creating from nothing. That is why only God is the One capable of being beautiful even on the cross. Thus Augustine observes, "Christ is beautiful wherever he is. He was beautiful in his miracles but just as beautiful under the scourges, beautiful as he invited us to life, but beautiful too in not shrinking from death, beautiful in laying down his life and beautiful in taking it up again, beautiful on the cross, beautiful in the tomb, and beautiful in heaven."

Through the centuries craftspeople and artists have been drawn to the task of depicting the crucifixion in paint, wood, and stone. No doubt they have done so with fear and trepidation. How do you show at once the terror and the beauty of God—a beauty so compelling we lose hold on our self-absorption? Yet the challenge has not deterred Christian and non-Christian artists alike from probing the mystery of the crucifixion. The cross draws the artist, as it does us, to contemplate the fittingness, the beauty, of the goodness of God.

Timothy Radcliffe, OP, observes that God's offer of forgiveness and reconciliation to us in the cross is not God forgetting Good Friday, because

> if forgiveness were forgetting then God would have to suffer the most acute amnesia, but it is God's unimaginable creativity, which takes what we have done and makes it fruitful. The medieval image of God's forgiveness was the flowering of the cross. The cross is the ugly sign of torture. It is the sign of humanity's ability to reject love and to do what is utterly sterile. But the artists of the Middle Ages showed this cross flowering on Easter Sunday. The dead wood put out tendrils and flowers. Forgiveness makes the dead live and the ugly beautiful.

Here is the beauty that defeats the ugliness of our lives. It does so because the beauty of the cross, in spite of our best efforts, refuses our sentimental attempts to explain the crucifixion. We are tempted (and we often try) to make what the Father has done through the sacrifice of the Son nothing but a confirmation of our presumption that we are the center of the universe. But the circle supporting the arms of this cross is a reminder that this cross determines the very character of the cosmos. God's new creation glows with the beauty of the stars, drawing us out of our self-imposed narcissism.

The cross, therefore, is not a symbol to explain inexplicable suffering. We do not need Jesus to explain or to contain our rage when faced by the tragedies of the world. Rather Jesus's cross is his alone, making possible a people who do not need an explanation for inexplicable suffering. Love, not explanation, is required when we are faced by the tragedies of life. Our task, a task made possible as well as demanded by the cross, is not to turn away when faced by the suffering of others who are often made all the more alien and frightening by their suffering. Rather our task is to be present to one another when there is quite literally nothing we can do to save ourselves or those we love from having to suffer.

The beauty of the cross is meant to beckon us into friendship with God. God, through the cross, refuses our refusal of friendship. Though he was in the form of God, he did not regard equality with God as something to be exploited. Rather he emptied himself, taking the form of a slave, being born in human likeness, even humbling himself being obedient to the point of death, even death on a cross, so that he might overwhelm our determined isolation and claim us as friends. And by claiming us, Christ makes friendship with one another a possibility and, perhaps, even friendship with ourselves.

It is particularly gratifying, therefore, that this processional cross is a witness to the friendship my wife, Paula, and I have been privileged to enjoy with the sculptor Bill Moore. Sixteen years ago we first saw some of his abstract marble sculptures. The beauty of his work drew us to him and to one another. Bill is an artist, a craftsman, and I am not. Bill's passion, the risks he must make to express his life in bronze and stone, frightens me. But I should like to think that this cross, Bill's willingness to handle Christ, in some small way is an expression of our love of one another.

So now let us come to the table, the table to which we have been led by this cross, the table where God welcomes us as friends, to handle his Christ. Here God invites us to share with him and one another the body and blood of Christ so that the world may know that we have been befriended. Come and see, come and taste, how right, how fitting, it is that in this meal God invites us to participate in, to be part of, the love, the beauty, that is the cross.

7

The End of Sacrifice

A Sermon for the Church of the Holy Family
Good Friday
March 25, 2005

Genesis 22
Psalm 22
Hebrews 10:1–25
John 19:1–37

"Then Pilate took Jesus and had him flogged." Some time has passed but the cinematic images of that lacerated body will not go away. As Jesus was beaten beyond what we think any human body could stand, we resist believing that our Lord so suffered. We refuse to believe that even the Romans could be that cruel. But they were that cruel. Whatever Mel Gibson's *The Passion of the Christ* may have done for helping us understand the crucifixion, at least the depiction of Jesus's suffering and death challenged our heretical tendency to assume that Jesus was less than fully human.

Yet that beating, that unending beating, also misleads. The cross cannot be isolated from the life that led to the crucifixion if we are rightly to understand the salvation wrought by the cross. The misleading character of the film is nicely exemplified by American evangelical Protestants who say as they leave the film, "I had no idea he had to suffer that much for my sins"—an odd sentiment in light of the Protestant insistence that the cross should be empty. Catholics are crucifix people—they enjoy suffering, thinking that sacrifices need to be made to be saved. Protestants are resurrection people. Protestants, accordingly, believe that sacrificial language on the whole should be avoided—thus our crosses are absent the body.

The assumption, however, that Jesus had to suffer, had to be sacrificed, for our sins is hard to repress even for Protestants. Some meaning must be gotten from this terror. The crucifixion account from the Gospel of John is too spare, too realistic: we want to know more. "There they crucified him." But why? The Jews accuse him of claiming to be a king, the Son of God, and that would warrant a death sentence. But a death so determined does not explain how that death benefits us. Does his crucifixion, as many Christians claim, have to do with our sins? Did a sacrifice need to be made for our sins? To avoid the language of sacrifice Protestants say a debt had to be paid, which often implies a view of God's justice as vengeance.

Even among more liberal Christians it is assumed that the crucifixion needs explanation and that such an explanation must have something to do with our sins. But we are not at all sure what to do with all this sacrificial language. We, that is, folks like you and me, try to make the crucifixion less sacrificial by saying that this is the form love must take in a cruel world. Yet we wonder—why does love have to suffer even to death? Why does a sacrifice need to be made for us to learn to love one another? And why on a cross?

Yet the sacrificial cross dominates our liturgical space. All we do every Sunday is centered on an altar of sacrifice. Our liturgy is dominated by the language of sacrifice. "He made there a full and perfect sacrifice for the whole world; and did institute, and in his holy gospel command us to continue, a perpetual memory of that, his precious death and sacrifice, until his coming again." Yet we remain puzzled—why the sacrifice of the cross? Why die at all? Why must a sacrifice be made? If God is

God, could not God simply say, "Listen, I have had enough of human malfunction. You people need to love one another. So I have sent Jesus to teach you how to get along."

We simply are not sure what to do with the language of sacrifice and the connection that language has with the cross. I fear we are tempted to think the cross is a symbol that exemplifies sacrifices characteristic of our everyday lives rather than the one unique sacrifice only God could make. Yet we worry that such a unique sacrifice—that is, a sacrifice only God can command and fulfill—is unworthy of God. If we are honest we should acknowledge that we think it profoundly immoral for God to ask Abraham to sacrifice Isaac. Moreover, even if the binding of Isaac is a story about the substitution of animals for child sacrifice (an interpretation I think quite doubtful), it is still the case that we do not think the sacrifice of animals, as a substitute for child sacrifice, is that much better. I fear we may believe that if biblical religion is a religion of sacrifice, it is best left behind—which means we must believe the Romans did a good thing when they destroyed the temple.

Such an attitude toward sacrifice marks us as modern. In the ancient world sacrifice was at the heart of all religious practice. The Old Testament prophets were quite critical of pagan sacrifices; but even pagan sacrifices, idolatrous though they were, at least witnessed to the pagan conviction that there was a god or gods to receive our sacrifices. Sacrifice, human and animal sacrifice, embodies the conviction that everything that is and all we are owes its existence to God. Only God can ask Abraham to sacrifice Isaac. Isaac may be Abraham and Sarah's son; but he is first and foremost God's gift to Abraham and Sarah. So to sacrifice Isaac was to give back to God what was God's own.

Isaac, moreover, is the exemplification of Israel's very existence. Do not forget that what God asked of Abraham was not just the sacrifice of his son, but to kill the child that represented God's promise that Abraham would be the father of a nation—a holy nation sanctified by a law through which she learned to live as God's people. Sacrifice was constitutive of such a people. Indeed the very existence of Israel was sacrificial, making possible the recognition of sin. Israel had been called to be a holy people, a people free from pollution, but not all sin could be

68

dealt with through individual repentance. Sacrifice at the altar became for Israel the way to expiate the sins of the whole people. Accordingly the temple in Jerusalem, which had at its center the altar of sacrifice, became the heart of Israel's existence.

We simply do not find persuasive these general anthropological and religious presumptions that shaped the practice of sacrifice in Israel. We think, moreover, that our rejection of sacrifice reflects criticism of sacrifice found in the Old and New Testaments. What the people of Israel came to realize is that God does not want blood sacrifice. Thus Psalm 51:15–17 says:

> O Lord, open my lips,
> and my mouth will declare your
> praise.
> For you have no delight in sacrifice;
> if I were to give a burnt offering
> you would not be pleased.
> The sacrifice acceptable to God is a
> broken spirit;
> a broken and contrite heart, O God,
> you will not despise.

The same attitude toward sacrifice is exemplified in Matthew 12:7. There Jesus responds to the Pharisees' criticism of the disciples for breaking the Sabbath by quoting Hosea 6:6 that God desires "steadfast love and not sacrifice, the knowledge of God rather than burnt offerings."

Our text from the book of Hebrews seems to stand in the tradition that calls for the end of sacrifice. In it we are told that "it is impossible for the blood of bulls and goats to take away sins." Consequently, when Christ came into the world, he said:

> Sacrifices and offerings you have not
> desired,
> but a body you have prepared
> for me;
> in burnt offerings and sin offerings
> you have taken no pleasure.

Then I said, "See God, I have come to
do your will, O God,
in the scroll of the book it is
written of me. . . . (Heb. 10:4–7)

As I noted we assume these texts legitimate our assumption that the language of sacrifice is best left in the past. But none of the passages I have just read suggest that a sacrifice is not required. God, it seems, still desires a sacrifice, the sacrifice suggested by Hebrews 10:5b, where Christ says, "a body you have prepared for me," a body, moreover, to be sacrificed. Thus the author of Hebrews says that by Jesus's death "a single offering" has been made, perfecting "for all time those who are sanctified." Holiness requires that a sacrifice be made. Indeed, the very meaning of sacrifice is "making holy." We believe a sacrifice has been made, the sacrifice of Christ's cross, that makes possible a people who can be for the world an alternative to the world's insistence on the need for sacrifice.

No doubt many would say we have left sacrificial systems behind, but that belief only hides from us that our lives are constituted by sacrifice. We sacrifice the lives of animals that we may live. We sacrifice our young in war that we may feel secure. We make sacrifices in the name of the love we feel for one another. We make sacrifices because too often we think that is the only way we can "make up" for the wrongs we have done. We think, though we seldom acknowledge that we do so, that God should take some notice of our sacrifices. Indeed we suspect that God, if he is the kind of god capable of meeting our needs, should credit our sacrifices.

The problem with these sacrificial systems is that too often they represent our attempts to avoid the reality that, as we read in Hebrews, Christ has "offered for all time a single sacrifice for sins." Indeed our text from Hebrews provides an acute analysis of our attempt to avoid the recognition that the sacrifice of the cross is the end of sacrifice. We are told that the law was only the shadow of the good things to come and, therefore, that the sacrifices of the law, the sacrifices offered year after year, could not make perfect the people offering them. The argument in the book of Hebrews suggests that those making such sacrifices could not be made perfect by the sacrifices because if their sacrifices were capable of freeing them from sin, then they would have needed to offer only one sacrifice. The very necessity of offering sacrifices year after year only served to remind those making sacrifices of their sins. Sin, not holiness, therefore continued to dominate their lives.

Ironically, those having seen Gibson's film who conclude (a quite understandable conclusion) that Jesus's suffering was an expiation for their sins make Christ's cross the kind of law that our text from Hebrews says cannot make us perfect. Sin, not cross and resurrection, dominates the narrative that makes Christ's sacrifice all about us. But according to Hebrews, Jesus abolished burnt offerings and sin offerings because it was the Father's will that we be "sanctified through the offering of the body of Jesus Christ once and for all." Through the sacrifice of Christ all our attempts to make our sacrifices matter is revealed to be sin. John Bunyan, assuming God's voice, writes, "Sinner, thou thinkest that because of thy sins and infirmities I cannot save thy soul, but behold my Son is by me, and upon him I look, and not on thee, and will deal with thee according as I am pleased with him."

Sacrifice is the preeminent human action that gestures our rightful desire to return to God. God created us to be animals that sacrifice. God tried to help us through the law rightly to sacrifice to him, but we are subtle creatures capable of making God's good gifts serve the devices and desires of our own hearts. Despite this, God joined his life to our life, becoming one of us, to free us from our attempt to be more than we were created to be. The Father sent the Son, humbled in human form, obedient to the point of death, even the death on a cross, to end forever any sacrifice not determined by his cross. Our Father restrained Abraham, providing a ram in place of Isaac; but the Father did not spare his only Son becoming for us the sacrifice necessary to free us from our endless attempts to atone for our sins on our own terms. That is why Good Friday, this day of agony and terror, is called "good."

Yet the goodness of this day, of this sacrifice, is not the goodness the world desires. This human being, as Pilate insisted, is a King who has put an end to all the sacrifices the leaders of this world use to give their rule the appearance of sanctity. Christ's sacrifice is the one true sacrifice calling into question all the sacrifices asked on behalf of lesser causes and lesser gods. That is why the rulers of this world—who war against the cross or try to co-opt it—finally must tremble before the cross. The cross of Christ challenges their very right to ask for sacrifices to be made on their behalf. That is why Augustine maintained that justice is to be found where God, the one supreme God, rules an obedient City according to his grace, forbidding any sacrifice to any being save himself alone.

The one sacrifice that is not forbidden, the one sacrifice that is required, is that sacrifice called Eucharist. The Father desires, as the book of Hebrews says, to have us "enter the sanctuary" made possible by the sacrificial flesh and blood of Jesus. Indeed we are made, through Christ's body and blood, God's sanctuary, God's holy temple, for the world. Just as this bread and wine is transformed by the Holy Spirit to be for us the body and blood of Christ, our lives, our everyday sacrifices, are taken up in this oblation. Through that transformation the sacrifices, so often forced upon us, can become life giving because they have an end.

Our sacrifices can be joined to Christ's sacrifice not because the Lord's sacrifice is insufficient, but because the sacrifice of the cross is complete, lacking nothing, sufficient for our salvation and the salvation of the world. The Eucharist is the self-offering of the church made possible by the self-offering of Christ. Time and time again we are given the good gift to participate in this, the Father's sacrifice of the Son, that all might know that here sacrifice has come to an end, because the cross is the end of all sacrifice. So on this dark day remember the painful sacrifice of the Son, a sacrifice in which we are made participants, and rejoice and be glad.

8

A Cross-Shattered Church

A Sermon for Duke Divinity School
in the University Chapel
February 2, 2005

Micah 6:1–8
Psalm 15
1 Corinthians 1:18–31
Matthew 5:1–12

Look around. Pick out those you do not think wise by human standards. Who are the morons, the ones who are really stupid? Would you raise your hand? Of course not all of you are stupid. Some of you are here because you did not have what it takes to make it in the world of power and influence. By going into the ministry, a debased profession in a debased institution, you will not be expected to be powerful. Moreover, few of you were (as we say in the South) born right. If you had been born to the right kind of people, you would have known you should go to law school.

What a motley group of people you are! Of course, for some there is the escape clause noticed by close readers, that is, those trained by Richard Hays.[1] Paul says "not many" of you were wise by worldly standards, "not many" were powerful, "not many" were of noble birth. So some of us have got to be that "not many." Of course, if we think we are the "not many," we have to disguise that we are the "not many" in order to avoid offending the stupid, weak, and not well born.

Which is a reminder that this business of being stupid, powerless, without nobility is tricky. Paul's criticism of the Corinthian church makes it impossible to avoid the knowledge that this is not exactly a lovely group of people who really like one another. No doubt Paul was trying to remind the Corinthians that the envy-fueled disunity of the world reflects habits built on the assumption that wisdom, power, and nobility are scarce resources. However, if the Corinthians are exemplifications of those lacking wisdom, power, and nobility, it is clear that lacking the worldly characteristics of wisdom, power, and nobility does not necessarily lead to a cooperative and unified community.

Let's face it: the emphasis Christians put on being weak, lacking in wisdom, power, and nobility is, as the philosophers like to say, counterfactual. Are you really supposed to lack worldly wisdom? If you are lacking in smarts, what in the world are you doing here? Think how hard you had to work to be admitted to the Divinity School. The Divinity School at Duke takes pride in the fact that we now turn down half our applicants. God may favor those who are not wise by worldly standards, but the Divinity School does not. Consider the new building. I do not think it would have been built without help from people with power and money. And surely, having money is what it means in our day to have been born right.

What, therefore, are we to make of this tension between the celebration of weakness and our need as Christians for knowledge, power, and money? Jesus tells his disciples that he is sending them out into the midst of wolves, requiring that they "be wise as serpents and innocent as doves" (Matt. 10:16). To be wise as serpents and innocent as doves (a species of bird that seems to me to be terminally stupid) is a formula for ongoing self-deception or, at least, false consciousness. You know the routine. You may be as smart as they come, you may work extremely hard, but you know when you are around Christians you had better play at being "just another good old boy." As a result passive-aggressive behavior becomes a way of life. We call the well-formed practitioners of that way of life "Methodist."

I think we need to go back to the beginning. Paul says that the message of the cross is foolishness to those who are perishing, but to those who are being saved it is the power of God. For "in the wisdom of God, the world did not know God through wisdom." God's calling us, those who are not wise, powerful, or nobly born, does not mean that the cross is not the embodiment of wisdom, power, and nobility. Nothing could be more reasonable, nothing could be more powerful, nothing could be nobler, than the salvation wrought in the cross. Thus John Howard Yoder's claim: "The cross is neither foolish nor weak, but natural."

"Natural?" What an odd claim. Yoder, the advocate of Christian nonviolence, claims that the cross is "natural." What could that possibly mean? For example, we think nonviolence names an ideal, a possibility that requires we ask how to get from here, a violent world, to there, a world of nonviolence. The form of the question suggests that nonviolence must be "unnatural," irrational, and that is why we have to work so hard to secure peace in a violent world—peace among even the people in the church in Corinth. Yoder suggests, however, that Jesus's cross challenges questions that ask how to get from here to there. The apocalyptic transformation of the world named by the cross means that the challenge is how the present world can be transformed to the reality that it already is. Thus we are not asked to love our enemies in order to make them our friends; but "we are called to act out of love for them because at the cross it has been effectively proclaimed that from all eternity they were our brothers and sisters. We are not called to make the bread of the world available to the hungry; we are called to restore the true awareness that it was always theirs."

Jesus's willingness to go to the cross is not simply the revelation of God's power and wisdom—the cross *is* the power and wisdom of God. Which means, according to Yoder, that Jesus's decision to go to the cross was "an ontological decision, dictated by a truer picture of what the world *really is*." Yoder even suggests (and remember this is an Anabaptist talking) that such an understanding of what Jesus did is reminiscent of Scholastic Christology; that is, Jesus is rightly understood as a king, just as he was a priest and a prophet, because he was the suffering servant. That story, moreover, means that the cross is the fundamental order of being and knowing because there is no more fundamental mode of reality.

But if the cross is the way the world is, then it means that those of you called to the ministry of the church have your work cut out for you. You may seem stupid in the eyes of the world; but if you are faithfully to serve the "there," then your lack of wisdom, power, and nobility must be cross-determined. That is why it is important that you had to work hard to be accepted to the Divinity School. That is why it is important that we have people, the "not many," who are able to make the new building possible. For if we are to be the wisdom the cross makes possible, then we must exemplify, we must be able to show, the difference that makes in the world in which we find ourselves. Which for us means the world of the university.

Clearly most of the knowledges that characterize this university or the universities in which you were educated are not disciplined by the wisdom of the cross. For example, ask yourself what would courses in international relations look like if they were taught from the perspective that the cross has abolished war. How would the explanatory modes in courses in economics be organized if it were assumed that life, and love, is not a zero-sum game? In biology how would organisms and their interrelation be understood if it were assumed that each creature is inadequately understood if the way it glorifies God is not constitutive of its being?

Just to the extent we think the wisdom of the cross does not require these extraordinary intellectual tasks, you have an indication that our stupidity is not cross-determined. It is, of course, true that any attempt to have the wisdom of the cross shape our understanding of the world—and in particular that part of the world called the university—is a daunting task. We are not sure even how to begin. We are almost certainly not smart enough for such an undertaking. Nor are we sure we possess the courage and humility required for the challenge to be a cross-shaped church.

But Paul tells us that is why we have been chosen. God chose the weak to shame the strong. So look around you. Expect to see those who are the poor in spirit, those who mourn, the meek, those who hunger and thirst for righteousness, the merciful, the pure in heart, peacemakers, and the persecuted. Jesus does not say that we should try to be poor in spirit, meek, merciful, persecuted. Rather he says that you should not be surprised that those called to serve in his cross-shaped kingdom will find among you those who have learned to do justice, love kindness, and walk humbly with God. You will need these gifts, moreover, if you are to be for the world an alternative to the world's wisdom. Only a community shaped by such a people—a people who have learned to rely on our different gifts—stands a chance of being for the world Jesus's cross-shaped wisdom. Only a people so constituted have a chance to produce knowledge that reflects that all that is is God's good creation.

So come to this meal of the new creation, this cross-determined meal, in which we are made God's wisdom through the work of the Holy Spirit. Again look around as you come, seeing in one another the wisdom of the cross and, so seeing, be glad. For what a joy it is that God has made of people like us—the stupid, the powerless, those lacking in nobility, and, even, the "not many"—his glory. Praise God.

Part III

LIVING

9

Death Undone

A Sermon for Saint Margaret's Episcopal Church
Winnipeg, Canada
Feast of All Saints
November 5, 2006

Isaiah 25:6–9
Psalm 24
Revelation 21:1–6
John 11:32–44

Jesus raised Lazarus from the dead, but that only delays the inevitable. Lazarus will still have to die one day. Which is a reminder that we too, like Lazarus, will have to die. Jesus said to Martha, "I am the resurrection and the life. Those who believe in me, even though they die, will live, and everyone who lives and believes in me will never die. Do you believe this?" Good question. Like Martha we say, "Yes, Lord, I believe that you are the Messiah, the Son of God, the one coming into the world," but that answer is evasive. We may believe Jesus is the resurrection and the life, but we know, like Lazarus, that we are going to die.

It is hard, moreover, for us to live in the light of Jesus's resurrection. Like Martha, we may believe Jesus is the Son of God, but I suspect the reality that we are destined to die means that we are not at all sure we know what we are saying when we say, "Yes, Lord, I believe you are the Messiah, the Son of God." I often observe that now that I am in my sixties I am beginning to realize that death is not a theoretical possibility— even for me. I am going to die. Yet as sure as my dying is, I am not at all sure I have comprehended or understood what it means for me to die. When I was young, that is, when I lived as if I would never die, I assumed when I was actually faced with death I would be frightened. I have discovered, however, that I so little understand what it means to die that I am more puzzled than frightened—at least I think I am more puzzled than frightened.

I was visiting a close friend, Tommy Langford, the day before he died. Tommy was a theologian, the former dean of the Divinity School at Duke who also served as the provost of the university. Tommy was one of those classical Southern Christian gentlemen who had a deep realism about the world yet did so without becoming cynical. He was thereby able to love most of the folk with which he came into contact. He had had a serious heart attack in his fifties, which meant he lived knowing every day could be his last. So he spent a great deal of time planting daffodils. During my visit, which I had no idea would be my last, I asked him if he was afraid to die. He said, "No, that would be a philosophical mistake, but I am going to miss my friends." Tommy had been deeply influenced by Wittgenstein so I assumed his suggesting that to be afraid to die was a philosophical mistake was an allusion to Wittgenstein's remarks in the *Tractatus*:

The world of the happy man is a different one from that of the unhappy man.

So too at death the world does not alter, but comes to an end.
Death is not an event in life: we do not live to experience death.

Wittgenstein's remarks may seem obscure, but in *The City of God* Augustine provides an analysis of the grammar surrounding death and comes to a conclusion quite similar to Wittgenstein's. Augustine observes that it is not clear how to describe that time when we hang suspended between life and death. He asks, "Are we to say that this period is *after* death or *in* death?" This leads Augustine to wonder what the implication of the preposition "after" or "in" might mean for whether death is good or evil: "If it is after death, then it is not the actual death, which is now past and gone, which is good or bad, but the present life of the soul after death. Death was evil for them, certainly at the time when it was present, that is when they were experiencing it in the act of dying, since it entailed a heavy burden of suffering—though the good make good use of that evil. But now that death is past, how can it be good or evil, since it no longer exists?"

Augustine argues, therefore, that a person who is dying must be living, which means it is very hard to define when someone is dying, "that is 'in death'; a state in which he is neither living (which is a state *before* death) or dead (which is *after* death), but dying, or 'in death.'" Augustine observes that he, therefore, finds it "significant and appropriate—though it happened not by human design, but perhaps by divine decision—that the grammarians have not been able to decline (or conjugate) the Latin verb *moritur* ('he dies') by the same rule as other verbs of this form." Even the grammar surrounding death seems to make it difficult for us to get a handle on dying or death.

Commenting on Augustine's reflections on the inability of our grammar to do justice to what it means for us to die, the theologian Robert Jenson observes that "humanity has found the sheer cessation of a person literally unthinkable, for death so conceived is the termination of consciousness, and that turns out to be an impossible thought." It is an impossible thought because "when I try to think of my own death as cessation, the best I can do is to think of myself as remembering that I used to be and so being conscious that I now am nothing and am conscious of nothing. To the concept of truly vanished consciousness, no projected experience can correspond."

I am sure this brief philosophical foray into the conceptual conundrums surrounding death has made you feel much better about the fact that before long, like me, you are going to be dead. The bottom line seems to be: do not worry about being dead because when you are dead you will not know you are dead. Does that not sound like good news? But if that is the case then we have to wonder about our texts for today and what they have to do, if anything, with All Saints.

Why, for example, are we told in Isaiah that the day is coming when the shroud that is cast over all people, the shroud of death, will forever be swallowed up? What is this shroud? Why, given our inability to imagine what it means for us to be dead, do we fear death so? In the book of Revelation we are told God will come to dwell among the mortals and death will be no more. But what is the death that is no more? Why, in 1 Corinthians 15:26, does Paul describe death as the last enemy to be destroyed?

The answer, of course, is that the death that is the last enemy to be destroyed, the shroud that death is, the death we rightly fear—this death is the death brought by sin. Augustine observes that the death we suffer because of Adam is in fact two deaths. The first is the death of the soul and the body, but the second death is the death due to sin, which has cut us off from God. Augustine thought this second death, the death due to sin, is what makes the first death of body and soul so frightening. For what we fear about death is not death per se; what we fear is the idea that death means an endless perpetuation of the loneliness that currently fuels our sinful attempts to be our own creator.

Tommy was, therefore, profoundly right to say that he was going to miss his friends. In light of this realization, however, we might learn to recognize death as a gift that makes friendship possible. For it is in embracing our finitude that we come to see how precious it is that we have been given the time to love and be loved. It is only from this perspective of time that death can be seen as gift insofar as it teaches us that our shared life together is pure gift. Yet at the same time death becomes our enemy because it threatens to rob us of our friendships. We rightly detest death, therefore, because it reminds us that our finitude requires that we be apart from each other. Which makes it even more important that we learn to die confident that God through Jesus Christ has overcome our enemy. Whether living or dead, in Christ we are united—we are not alone.

An American evangelical philosopher once asked me if I did not think that hell is best conceived as being hated by God. I responded by saying that is surely wrong. If I know I am hated by God, I at least know I exist. Hell is to be abandoned by God. Dante surely had it right that at its lowest depths hell is where we are frozen in ice in a manner that those so condemned are unable to see anyone else.

Robert Jenson puts it this way:

> What makes death the Lord's enemy, and fearful for us, is that it separates lovers. Were my death simply my affair, the old maxim might hold, that since my death will never be part of my experience, I have no need to fear it. But death will take my loves from me and me from them, and that is the final objective horror, for it decrees emptiness of all human worth, constituted as it is by love. Having no more being would be no evil were being not mutual.

But being is mutual, because mutuality is the very character of God—Father, Son, and Holy Spirit. The Father desires friendship with the Son through the agency of the Holy Spirit. Which means speculation about dying and death that is not governed by Jesus's cross and resurrection only tempts us to narcissistic fantasies. What we know is that the crucified Jesus has been raised, making possible our hope that death cannot defeat God's love for us. We were created for God's enjoyment and through the Son's obedience even to death he has reclaimed us so that we may regard our deaths not as an end but as a beginning. In short God does not give us explanations that can make our dying something less than death. He does not give us an explanation; he gives us his Son.

It is often said that when all is said and done we will each have to die alone. But that is the shroud, that is the death, that we believe has been swallowed up by Christ. We do not have to die alone, but rather we die believing that Christ has gone before us. That is why it is appropriate that we confront death as part of the celebration of All Saints. We stand in awe of the martyrs' willingness to face death, but the martyrs do not seem to make much of their dying. I think they do not make much of their dying, indeed they do not even make much of how they must die, because death does not dominate their dying. Their attention is not captured by their dying or death, but rather "they do see Jesus." Indeed they often even ask that we not grieve their death, but rather their sin, because the death they die is one shaped by Jesus having claimed them as his friend.

Augustine observes:

> Therefore the death of the saints is precious (Psalm 116, 15) the saints for whom the death of Christ was the price already paid in advance. And such grace came from Christ's death that to gain him they did not hesitate to pay the price of their own death, the death that showed that what had been imposed as the penalty for sin had been turned to such good use that it brought to birth a richer harvest of righteousness. Death, therefore, ought not to be rewarded as a good thing because it has been turned to such good advantage. For this happened not in virtue of any quality of its own, but by the help of God; so that death, which was put forward as a fearful warning against sin, is now set before men as something to be accepted when that acceptance means the avoidance of sin and the cancellation of sins committed, and the reward of the palm of victory as the just reward of righteousness.

So Martha's answer, "Yes, Lord, I believe that you are the Messiah, the Son of God, the one coming into the world," was not an evasion but a declaration of reality. That reality is exemplified in the lives of the saints who teach us how to die. Most of us will not die martyrs' deaths, but the deaths martyrs die help us die gentle deaths. For why should we shrink, the Irish poet Monk Gibbon asks, from "this little door"? And to this he answers:

> O fools shrinking
> From this little door,
> Through which so many kind and lovely souls have passed
>   before you,
>   Will you hang back?
> Harder in your case than another?
>   Not so.
> And too much silence?
> Has there not been enough stir here?
>   Go bravely,

For where so much greatness and
  Gentleness have been already,
  You should be glad to follow.

We live in a death-denying world that seems determined to develop technologies that will enable us to get out of life alive. Yet the more we strive to be free of death the more our lives are shaped by the death-determined means we create to try to free ourselves of death. Even more paradoxical, the means we use to free ourselves from death only serve to increase our isolation from one another. We fear the loneliness we think death entails, but it turns out that the loneliness we fear death entails is the expression of the loneliness made unavoidable by our attempts to avoid death.

Jesus raised his friend Lazarus from the dead. But Lazarus is still to die. We are still to die. Jesus, by contrast, has been raised never again to die. His death makes possible a communion that overwhelms the loneliness our sin creates. Our God has made his home among the mortals by assuming our deadly flesh so that we might be made friends of Jesus and even one another. Such friendship means we rightly mourn the loss of friends, yet we can rejoice in the knowledge that the living and the dead share the common reality of this new city, a city of the martyrs, the New Jerusalem.

For we believe that God has in fact prepared for his people a feast of rich food and wine. That feast we call Eucharist, for in eating it we are made "living members of your Son our Savior Jesus Christ." We believe, moreover, that when we celebrate this holy meal we do so with the saints who have gone before and who now share in God's eternal life. The devil would have us remain fixated on death, but in sharing this meal we learn to gaze upon Christ, who makes it possible to view our lives and deaths through the power of the resurrection. Death has been undone.

10

Only Fear Can Drive Out Fear

A Sermon for the Church of the Holy Family
July 9, 2006

Ezekiel 2:1–7
Psalm 123
2 Corinthians 12:1–10
Mark 6:1–6

In the "Great Litany" of the Episcopal Church, we pray to be delivered "from all oppression, conspiracy, and rebellion; from violence, battle, and murder; and from dying suddenly and unprepared." Wait a minute—do we want to pray to be delivered from a sudden death? Most of us, I suspect, want to die quickly, in our sleep, painlessly, and without being a burden. We do not want to be a burden because we are not at all sure we can trust our children to make decisions about our care. We want to die quickly, in our sleep, and painlessly because when we die we do not want to know we are dying. We, therefore, want doctors to keep us alive to the point that when we die we do not have to know we are dying. We then get to blame doctors for keeping us alive to no point.

It is quite interesting to ask what accounts for the difference between our attitude toward death and those of Christians in earlier centuries, who thought they should pray to be delivered from a sudden death. I think the answer is quite simple—they prayed to be delivered from a sudden death because they feared God, not death. Our prayer book has several prayers that reflect the "Great Litany" prayer, prayers that suggest as we die we need to prepare to face God. For example, the prayer entitled, "For the Sanctification of Illness" reads: "Sanctify, O Lord, the sickness of your servant, that the sense of her weakness may add strength to her faith and seriousness to her repentance; and grant that she may live with you in everlasting life; through Jesus Christ our Lord. Amen." I think it not accidental, moreover, that in the Book of Common Prayer the "Reconciliation of a Penitent" is immediately followed by "Ministrations to the Sick."

Those who, across many centuries, prayed to be delivered from a sudden death did so because they did not want to face God's judgment unprepared. They wanted to be forgiven for their sins. They wanted time to be reconciled with their enemies, the church, and God. Yet we find prayers like "For the Sanctification of Illness" hard to pray because we do not like to think the God we may or may not face after death will be a judge. As a result our lives are determined by our fear of death. Of course we live in denial of our fear of death. Yet think about the widespread belief that through research modern medicine will finally make it possible for us to get out of life alive.

This attitude toward death, moreover, is the reason that medical education is a more serious form of moral education than the training we give people going into the priesthood. After a short time in divinity school a student may say, "I am just not into Christology this year. I really want to help people, so I want to take more courses in Clinical Pastoral Education so that I will know better how to relate." In many divinity schools, though I am happy to say not the Divinity School at Duke, students are too often allowed to do just that. In contrast, a student in medical school might say, "I am not really interested in anatomy. I am really interested in relating to patients, so I would like to take more courses in psychiatry." That medical student would be told,

"We are not interested in what you are interested in. Take anatomy or ship out."

Medical education, therefore, entails a moral formation that those who teach in divinity schools can only envy. Why are those who run medical schools able to form students to be physicians in a manner we are not able to train students in divinity schools? Again I think the answer is quite simple: in this day few think that an inadequately trained minister may damage their salvation, but we do believe an inadequately trained doctor may hurt us. Accordingly we often care a great deal more who our doctor is than who our priest may be. This is but one example of how our everyday habits are shaped by fear—it is precisely because they are everyday habits that we do not notice our lives are fear driven.

We do live in a fear-driven country. After September 11, 2001, America is a country governed by fear. We are told we are the strongest and freest people in the world. Yet it seems that our strength only makes us vulnerable, requiring that we acquire more power in order to protect the power we have. Americans want to be safe. Americans want to be secure. But we live in a dangerous world. So Americans would have the rest of the world live in danger so that we may be a people who do not have to acknowledge, when all is said and done, that we will all be dead.

I recognize that what I have said about our fear of death may be exaggerated, but I suspect the very discomfort I feel saying what I have just said, as well as the discomfort I suspect you feel hearing what I have said, is an indication that there is some truth in what I have said. We would prefer not to acknowledge that our lives are shaped by fear, and, in particular, the fear of death. Moreover, even if such is the case it does little good to direct attention to the fears that shape our lives. You do not get over being afraid by trying not to be afraid. Indeed we usually find that attempts to will our way out of being afraid only make us all the more fearful.

Let us thank God, therefore, that God would have us fear him—and that by fearing him, as Psalm 111 tells us, we might begin to recognize as foolishness the fears that characterize the powers of this world. For only the fear of God can drive out the fears that enslave us. On October 22, 1978, John Paul II began his papacy with Christ's words, "Be not afraid." A Polish priest, who had survived the Nazis and communism, began his papacy by telling us we have nothing to fear because the Father has befriended us through the Son. The wonder, the sheer miracle of that befriending, overwhelms us. Such an overwhelming means that the fear of the Lord, a fear shaped by the sheer beauty of God, drives out all other fears that threaten to possess our lives.

God addresses Ezekiel, "O mortal," indicating clearly that Ezekiel is going to die. The prophet is a mortal, but one possessed by the very Word of God. Thus Ezekiel reports that when God spoke to him, "a spirit entered into him, setting him on his feet" so that he might be sent to Israel, a nation of rebels. God, moreover, leaves Ezekiel with no illusions about what God has told him to do. Indeed Ezekiel has much to fear because what God has given him to say, the people will refuse to hear. Instead these people will condemn the prophet, making his life akin to living in a briar patch, and beset by scorpions. But the prophet is not to be afraid of the words they use to condemn and ridicule him, nor is he to fear how they look at him. Overwhelmed by the spirit and, therefore, unafraid to say "thus says the Lord God," Ezekiel will at least make plain to all that a prophet has been among them.

To have our fears overwhelmed by the fear of God means that, like Ezekiel, our lives will never be the same. But that is exactly what the people of Nazareth refused to embrace in response to Jesus's teaching. Notice in our Gospel for today that the people of Nazareth were not ignorant. Many were astonished when Jesus began to teach in the synagogue. They recognized that what he was saying was extraordinary. They recognized that his teaching and his deeds of power could not be accounted for by their everyday modes of explanation: "What is this wisdom that has been given to him?" They clearly sense that Jesus has been given gifts that cannot be explained in terms of the everyday.

So they do what we would do. Rather than have their fears, fears that make the everyday "work," overwhelmed by the fear of the One who has the power to redeem, they resort to the normal. "Is not this the carpenter, the son of Mary, whose brothers and sisters we know well?" A response not unlike ours when asked to explain what it means to be a Christian—"Well, we all need to believe in something and Jesus seems, on the whole, to have recommended a good way to live." Which means that, like the people of Nazareth, we would rather die in our dread than face the cross of Christ and have our illusions die. For what is our deepest fear? That if we learned the truth about ourselves we could not live.

That is why we prefer to have a god who keeps his distance so that we might get on with our fear-determined lives. But Jesus comes to us as one of us. Our flesh is his hometown. We fear such a God, but only the One who has come among us as one of us can invade our lives so that our fears might be transformed by love. After his resurrection Jesus had to tell his disciples not to be afraid, because they were not sure if the one resurrected was the same Jesus they had followed (Matt. 28:10). That the disciples were afraid is quite understandable. To learn to see that the one crucified is the one resurrected means that the world as they and we know it will never be the same. It can no longer be the world created and sustained by our fear of death.

In *Crossing the Threshold of Hope*, John Paul II reflects on his first sermon as Pope, asking:

> Why should we have no fear? Because man has been redeemed by God. When pronouncing these words in St. Peter's Square, I already knew that my first encyclical and my entire papacy would be tied to the truth of the Redemption. In the Redemption we find the most profound basis for the words "Be not afraid!": "For God so loved the world that he gave his only Son" (John 3:16). This Son is always present in the history of humanity as Redeemer. It is the light that "shines in the darkness, and the darkness has not overcome it." (John 1:5) The power of Christ's Cross and Resurrection is greater than any evil which man could or should fear.

At Nazareth, because of the Nazarenes' unbelief, Jesus could do no deed of power except that he laid his hands on a few of the sick and cured them. Jesus's love for us is evident because he refuses to let our fears, our unbelief, prevent him from the deed of power his resurrection makes possible. We call that deed Eucharist. In the Eucharist our fears are overwhelmed by the power of God's love in Jesus, making it possible for us to be a spirit-filled people who can be an alternative to a world driven by fear. To be such a people does not mean that we may not end up amid the briars and stung by scorpions. What it does mean is that we will not fear those who would use words and looks of derision because of our refusal to lead death-determined lives. Jesus told us that prophets are seldom honored among their own. Yet let us hope that through this meal the world may at least recognize that by what is done here "there continues to be a prophet among us." So come to this table and "do not be afraid."

11

The Appeal of Judas

A Sermon for Duke Divinity School
March 28, 2007

Isaiah 43:16–21
Psalm 126
Philippians 3:4b–14
John 12:1–8

We are well-schooled Christians. We know that we are not to identify with Judas. Yet we cannot help but think, thief though he was, Judas was right—the costly perfume should have been sold and the money given to the poor. If we are honest we cannot resist the conclusion: Judas is appealing.

Moreover, if any conviction characterizes what it means to be a Christian in our day, it is surely the presumption that we ought to be on the side of the poor. No longer sure we know what it means to believe that Jesus is the Son of God, we at least take comfort that to be a Christian requires that we care about those less well off. Of course what it means for us—that is, for the moderately well off—to care for the poor usually extends no farther than our attempt to make the poor like us, that is, moderately well off.

Given the world in which we find ourselves, a world that thinks what Christians believe must make us doubtful allies in the struggle for justice, the Christian concern for the poor can win us some respect. The cultural despisers of the church at least have to acknowledge that Christians do some good in spite of our reactionary convictions. So it is good that we burn with a passion for justice. The only problem with such a passion is it can put us on Judas's side.

This means we are profoundly troubled if not offended by Jesus's response to Judas: "Leave her alone. She bought it so that she might keep it for the day of my burial. You will always have the poor with you, but you will not always have me." We wish Jesus had not said that. If you needed a text to confirm Marx's contention that Christianity is the opiate for the masses you need look no further than, "You always have the poor with you."

Yet note: the one who said "You always have the poor with you" was poor himself. That Mary saw fit to bestow a lavish gift on a poor person, a poor person who was soon to die, is sure to be celebrated—particularly by the poor. One of their own receives a lavish gift. One of their own is celebrated. So, if you are poor, what Mary does is a good.

It is of course true that Christians have used this text to teach the poor to accept their status by suggesting if they do so they will ultimately receive a greater reward than those well off. The church has also glossed over Jesus's response to Judas by not asking, "What if we did more than care for the poor?" or, "What if we celebrated the poor?"

That such questions are not asked reflects a church that has forgotten that Christianity is determinatively the faith of the poor. That is why we, the moderately well off, are puzzled by the undeniable reality that the church across time and space has been constituted by the poor. We, the moderately well off, are tempted to think, in response to Mary's gift, "What a waste." Surely a more utilitarian gift would have been more appropriate. But the poor know this is Jesus, the one who shares their lot, so what could be more appropriate than this lavish gift, bestowed on this man to prepare his body for death?

It is crucial that we notice this is a dinner where death is as present as those feasting. Lazarus, who had been raised from the dead, is present. But the resurrection of Lazarus only postpones the inevitable—Lazarus, like you and me, will die. Moreover, Mary's anointing presages Jesus's death. Mary had bought the perfume for the day of his death, but it seems she could not wait. And so she anoints him in order to prepare him for death.

I think it is not accidental that death and poverty are connected at this dinner. Death, after all, creates an economy of scarcity. We only have a few years to live. We cannot do everything we would like to do before we die. That some of us have been given more than others is just the way things have worked out. We do not necessarily want to be selfish but there is just so much that one can do in a world of limited resources.

Mary seems, however, to have caught a glimpse of a different world when Jesus raised Lazarus from the dead. Mary's gift, her outrageous gesture of love, indicates that she has been drawn into the abundance of God's kingdom, enacted by the life and death of the one who has said he is the resurrection and the life. She knows there is always "enough" because we cannot use Jesus up. In the Book of Common Prayer we pray this prayer for a monk:

> O God, whose blessed Son became poor that we through his poverty might be rich: Deliver us from an inordinate love of this world, that we, inspired by the devotion of your servant may serve you with singleness of heart, and attain to the riches of the age to come; through Jesus Christ our Lord, who lives and reigns with you, in the unity of the Holy Spirit, one God, now and for ever.

You know you are in a different world than the world of scarcity when you are a part of a people who can call monks rich. The grammar of this prayer, a grammar that must be written on the habit of our hearts, is crucial if we are to resist the appeal of Judas. Mary's extravagant gesture turns out to be what God has done for us, that is, lavish us with a love we cannot use up. But even more startling, we turn out to be the gift God would give the world through the work of the Holy Spirit.

That is why we must think of the wealth of the church as the wealth of the poor. The beauty of the cathedral is a beauty for the poor. The church's liturgy, her music and hymns, is a beauty of and for the poor. The literature of the church, her theology and philosophy, is distorted if it does not contribute to the common life determined by the worship of a Savior who was poor. The church's wealth, Mary's precious ointment, can never be used up or wasted on the poor.

No doubt such an account of the church's wealth can be an invitation to self-deception and justification for us, the moderately well off, not to hear the call of those in need. Yet "the poor you will always have with you" is not a description to legitimate a lack of concern for the poor. Rather, it is a description of a church that has learned "insofar as you do it to the least of these, you do it unto me." The church is that reenactment of Mary's lavish gift-giving pouring out ourselves for the world and therefore Christ.

Prudentius, a Christian poet and contemporary of Ambrose, celebrated the life of Saint Lawrence. Lawrence was a deacon in the Church of Rome in the middle of the third century. Lawrence was responsible for watching over the treasury of the church of San Lorenzo. The prefect of Rome had heard that Christian priests offered sacrifices in vessels of gold and silver and commended Lawrence to place before him the church's wealth. According to Prudentius, Lawrence replied:

> Our church is rich.
> I deny it not.
> Much wealth and gold it has
> No one in the world has more.

Accordingly, Lawrence promised to bring forth all the "precious possessions of Christ" if the prefect would give him three days to gather the church's wealth. Given the three days, Lawrence used them to gather the sick and the poor.

> The people he collected included a man with two eyeless sockets, a cripple with a broken knee, a one-legged man, a person with one leg shorter than the other, and others with grave infirmities. He writes down their names

and lines them up at the entrance of the church. Only then does he seek out the prefect to bring him to the church. When the prefect enters the doors of the church, Lawrence points to the ragged company and says, "These are the church's riches; take them." Enraged at being mocked, the prefect orders Lawrence to be executed slowly by being roasted on a gridiron.

Lawrence exemplifies what it means for the church always to have the poor with us. To have the poor with us, to have Jesus with us, does not mean our task is to make the poor rich. Of course, rich and poor Christians are called to serve one another. Rich and poor alike are called to feed the hungry and clothe the naked. But the church, if it is the church of the poor, must refuse the bargain with death that tempts us to live as if life is a zero-sum game of winners and losers. We are, after all, Mary's people, who have touched and have been touched by Jesus. And so we know, like Mary, that through Christ our lives have been opened up to the life of abundance. For Jesus, through his death and resurrection, is that abundance to which there is no end.

I am quite well aware that some may find what I have said to be "idealistic." Yet in a moment we will again eat and drink with the poor one who has invited us to share his body and blood. This is the gift of abundance. This is the gift that makes possible a people capable of sharing with one another. This is the gift that makes possible a people who have time for one another. This is the gift that challenges the presumptions of power, prestige, and status we think necessary to be of service to the poor. This is the reality that makes it possible to resist the appeal of Judas. So come and receive this lavish gift, and by receiving may we become poor so that the world might see what it means to be rich.

12

Slavery as Salvation

A Sermon for the Church of the Holy Family
March 2, 2008

Jeremiah 3:21–4:2
1 Corinthians 7:17–23
Mark 1:14–20
Psalm 130

Were you a slave when called? Do not be concerned about it." Jesus, we wish Paul had not said that. Did he really think being a slave was no problem? What a profoundly offensive position. What a profoundly offensive position for us who live "after slavery." The Civil War was horrid, but it at least ended slavery. Slavery may still exist, but we know it is wrong. That we know slavery is wrong is a moral achievement that we rightly believe makes us better people. Yet Paul, an apostle of Christ, does not seem to share our view that slavery is clearly incompatible with what it means to be a human being.

We know, moreover, that Paul means what he says because he sends the slave, Onesimus, back to Philemon. Paul is in prison. Onesimus has obviously been a crucial aid to Paul in prison. Paul even says that he regards Onesimus as his child. But he nonetheless sends Onesimus back to Philemon because he is Philemon's slave. To be sure, Paul asks Philemon to receive Onesimus back as "a beloved brother." Paul even suggests that Philemon should welcome Onesimus as he would Paul himself. But Paul does not ask Philemon to free Onesimus.

The scholar Dale Martin has written a wonderful book, entitled *Slavery as Salvation*, that helps us understand the complex reality of slavery in the ancient world. Slaves often held managerial positions that conferred status on those who held such offices. Accordingly Martin suggests that Paul's rhetoric surrounding slavery in 1 Corinthians can be interpreted as a form of upward mobility. Martin observes, however, that no one in the ancient world, if they could avoid it, would have wanted to be a slave. If you were a slave there were forms of slavery better than others, but who would want to be a slave? Yet Paul seems to imply that slavery for Christians is not a problem.

Nor are we helped by reading Paul's counsel about slavery in the wider context of 1 Corinthians. Paul's remarks about slavery are but one aspect of his general admonition to the Corinthians that becoming Christian does not entail radically trying to change their place in life. If they were married when they became a Christian they should stay married. If they were unmarried, stay unmarried. If they were uncircumcised, then stay uncircumcised. "Let each of you remain in the condition in which you were called." Not exactly a revolutionary doctrine. Could it be that Marx was right? That is, that Christianity is the opiate of the masses, designed to make the oppressed happy with their earthly lot by focusing their hopes on the life to come?

Of course Paul does tell those who may be slaves that if a chance for liberty should come they should take it. Moreover he says that whoever was a slave when they were called is now a free person belonging to the Lord. And whoever was a free person when they were called, Paul says, is now a slave of Christ. Yet that does not sound like good news. Onesimus is still Philemon's slave. Philemon may now be a slave of Christ and Onesimus may now be free in Christ, but what good is such a freedom or slavery if that freedom or that slavery has no outward effect? Paul's "rule" that we are to remain as we were seems to spiritualize the gospel in a manner that makes it good news only for those in power. I am not sure what good it does, for example, to tell those who are in power, those who are rich or have social or political status, that they are really slaves of Christ.

For many of us a Christianity that makes no earthly difference is profoundly offensive. No longer sure that what we believe as Christians is true, we at least want to claim that Christianity represents moral positions that are progressive. We want the church to make a difference. What good is what we do here Sunday after Sunday if what we do does not mobilize us to work to end the injustices that continue to grip our lives? "Let each of you remain in the condition in which you were called" does not sound like the difference we want the church to make.

However, this is but a reminder of our distance from Paul. Paul does not think that the church has to make a difference. Rather, for Paul, Christians must learn how to live in the light of the difference Jesus has made. That difference is named quite clearly in our Gospel: "Now after John was arrested, Jesus came to Galilee, proclaiming the good news of God, and saying, 'The time is fulfilled, and the kingdom of God has come near; repent and believe the good news.'" The world has been turned upside down because God has redeemed time by entering our time. The difference has come and his name is Jesus.

That difference, that name, is one that challenges the thrones and dominions of this world. The powers, moreover, know they are under attack. Otherwise why is John in jail? Why is Paul in jail when he writes to Philemon? Why was Martin Luther King Jr. in jail when he wrote his letter from Birmingham? "Repent, and believe the good news" is the radical proclamation that Jesus has unleashed a movement that puts in jeopardy the powers of this world, powers that gain their power from our fears of death and one another. Is it any wonder that we are rightly frightened by Jesus's call to repent and believe this good news?

We would like at the very least a moment to think about whether we want to join this movement. But Jesus gives those he calls no time to "make up their minds." He calls Simon and Andrew while they are at work, telling them he will make them fish for people. That they immediately leave their nets cannot strike us as anything but irresponsible.

101

How will they make a living? Simon is married. Surely his familial responsibilities should have trumped Jesus's call. Jesus goes a little further and sees James and John, the sons of Zebedee, mending their nets and he "immediately" calls them. They left the boat and, more important, their father and followed Jesus. It seems the difference Jesus is means that the everyday can no longer be presumed as a given. The family is no longer the first priority. The normal is no longer normative. The everyday is radically called into question—an everyday, for example, like the war in Iraq, justified in the name of protecting everyday responsibilities to family, nation, and all we associate with the American way of life. That everyday is now no longer normal given the difference Jesus is.

The difference Jesus inaugurates, the difference presupposed by the call of the disciples, is the difference and call Paul takes as a given when he tells the Corinthians to remain as they were before they were called. They can remain in the position in which they find themselves, not because nothing has changed, but because everything has changed. Note that Paul reminds the Corinthians, "You were bought with a price; do not become slaves of human masters. In whatever condition you were called, brothers and sisters, there remain with God." "Brothers and sisters?" Paul reminds the Corinthians they are brothers and sisters. They are now members of a new family, which means they may well be asked to leave nets, spouses—that is, the "normal"—to follow Jesus.

Consider, for example, Paul's rhetoric in his letter to Philemon. Paul charges Philemon to receive Onesimus "no longer as a slave but more than a slave, a beloved brother—especially to me but how much more to you, both in flesh and in the Lord." Paul, moreover, not so subtly reminds Philemon that Philemon owes his very life to Paul—that is, his salvation—so that any debt Onesimus might owe to Philemon should be forgiven, just as Paul forgives Philemon's debt to him.

"Brothers and sisters" denotes the new reality constituted by the movement made possible by Jesus's announcement that time is now fulfilled. The name of that new reality is "church." Jesus called the disciples to be apostles so that they could call us to be participants in the new age. A people have been brought into existence across time and space so that the world may know through the work of the Holy Spirit what

102

Jesus has done. The powers of domination have been defeated, having been exposed at the crucifixion as mere pretenders lacking substance. Christians, followers of Jesus, can remain in the conditions in which we find ourselves because we are a people constituted by a new way of life that saves us from those forms of life fueled by pretensions of status and power. Few slave owners desire to have slaves so formed.

Christians hunger and thirst for righteousness and justice, but we are not utopians. Failing to achieve their ideals, utopians and idealists too easily become cynics who, in their frustration, are willing to kill in the name of a good cause. Christians are revolutionaries, but we believe the revolution has happened and we are it. John Howard Yoder observes in *For the Nations* that "the real revolutions which change the nature of an entire civilization are those that take place in secret. They are those shifts in moral assumptions and in the availability of quality people which can take place only patiently and without notice" (118). Accordingly Yoder argues that the revolution in race relations in America over the past decades happened not because of the outworking of democratic ideals, but "by training strong personalities whose demeanor and whose gifts are even in silence a condemnation of those social structures which deny them their place."

"Remain in the condition in which you were called" does not mean, therefore, that such a condition is assumed legitimate or is to be accepted. The Emancipation Proclamation was enacted January 1, 1863, but it did not get to Texas until June 19, 1865. African-Americans in Texas celebrated that date simply by refusing to work on the nineteenth of June. They did so even though Juneteenth, as the day was known in Texas, was not an official holiday. Yet whites and African-Americans in Texas, at least the Texas in which I grew up, knew Juneteenth was the celebration of a freedom still to be realized. No one, black or white, worked on Juneteenth. African-Americans did not work because they were celebrating. Whites did not work because their work depended on the work of African-Americans.

We, the church of Jesus Christ, are God's Juneteenth. We are also Americans, the freest people in the world, or at least so we are told we are by the political leaders we have allegedly chosen to rule us. Let us

103

confess as Americans that we are not sure what it means for us to be made slaves of Christ. Let us admit we are not sure what it means for us to be God's Juneteenth. But at the very least I think it means that we should be ready to be surprised by what God may do to us and with us. We thought we would just show up another Sunday to hear the word and to share a meal, but before you know it we may find ourselves supporting Christians in jail because they are Christians. Being the church of Jesus Christ could get us, just as it got John the Baptist and Paul, in trouble. Coming to church could be dangerous. Before all this is over we, even we Americans, if we are slaves to Christ, could end up in jail. By God, sisters and brothers, being Christian turns out to be more interesting than we had imagined, but that is why "the difference" is such good news.

13

True Gentleness

A Sermon for the Church of the Holy Family
December 17, 2006

Zephaniah 3:14–20
Psalm 85:7–13
Philippians 4:4–9
Luke 3:7–18

L et your gentleness be known to everyone"—good advice, comforting advice, unremarkable advice. We often find Paul a bit hard to take, but his commendation of gentleness cannot help but strike us as a good idea. When you live, as most of us do, in relative comfort; when you know, as most of us do, that your life is relatively safe; when you are surrounded by relatively like-minded people as we are here at Holy Family, you cannot help but think that gentleness is a good idea. In like manner we think Paul's list of virtues—truth, honor, justice, purity—also names habits that most people believe you ought to try to develop.

We, therefore, hear Paul's recommendation of these virtues as confirmation of the widespread assumption that what it means to be a

Christian is pretty much the same thing as what it means to be a good person. Indeed we are a bit embarrassed by Christians who claim that being a Christian makes them different from those who are not Christian. Any suggestion that being a Christian involves a distinctive way of life that might distinguish Christians from those who are not is profoundly offensive to our democratic sensibilities. When it is all said and done, we believe that there is not that much difference between Christians and non-Christians. We all know, for example, people—oftentimes friends—who are not Christians but who live better lives than we do.

Our Gospel for today seems to confirm our presumption that a commonsense morality exists, which means Christians and non-Christians are basically the same. Thus, when tax collectors asked John the Baptist what they should do, he told them that they should be honest by taking no more than their due. No special insight is required for such a recommendation. In a similar fashion he told the soldiers to be satisfied with their wages, which meant they should not use force to extort money from those who could not protect themselves. John's suggestion to the crowd that if they have two coats they should share one with those who have none seems a little extreme, but most people recognize that sharing what we have with those less well off is a good thing. So the "fruits worthy of repentance" John says we must bear seem to be commensurate with what most of us think of as common sense morality.

There is just one problem with this way of reading Paul's commendation of gentleness, truth, honor, justice, and purity: namely, that he is writing from jail. If these characteristics are the "fruits worthy of repentance," if the virtues Paul recommends are generally recognized as a "good thing," how in the hell did Paul get himself arrested? Moreover, he is not even upset he is in jail because he says his imprisonment "has actually helped to spread the gospel, so that it has become known throughout the whole imperial guard and to everyone else that my imprisonment is for Christ; and most of the brothers and sisters having been made confident in the Lord by my imprisonment, dare to speak the word with greater boldness and without fear" (Phil. 1:12–14). The irrepressible Paul makes it hard to know who to feel more sorry for— Paul or his jailers.

That Paul is in jail challenges our assumption that his recommendation of gentleness, truth, honor, justice, and purity is as innocent as we assume. For it is easy, indeed it is tempting, to overlook Paul's admonition to the Philippians that they should "keep on doing the things that you have learned and received and heard and seen in me, and the God of peace will be with you." "Seen in me"? Paul seems to be suggesting we do not know what gentleness, truth, honor, justice, and purity entail if we have not seen these virtues "in him." And he is in jail. Indeed earlier in the letter to the Philippians Paul even tells the Philippians that they should

> join in imitating me, and observe those who live according to the example you have in us. For many live as enemies of the cross of Christ; I have told you of them, and now I tell you even with tears. Their end is destruction; their god is the belly; and their glory is in their shame; their minds are set on earthly things. But our citizenship is in heaven, and it is from there that we are expecting a Savior, the Lord Jesus Christ. He will transform the body of our humiliation that it may be confirmed to the body of his glory, by the power that also enables him to make all things subject to himself. (Phil. 3:17–20)

We cannot help but feel a bit uncomfortable with Paul's appeal to the Philippians that they should "imitate me" if that means, as we suspect it does, that we should live in a manner that others might imitate us imitating Paul. Interestingly enough, however, Paul's call to be imitated would not have surprised anyone in the ancient world. For it was presupposed by all philosophical schools that to become good, to acquire the virtues, required learning to imitate a master. Only by being apprenticed to a master could you learn to be good, not only by doing what a good person does, but by doing what is done in the way it must be done by a good person. Thus Aristotle's claim that "the just and temperate person is not the one who merely does these [just or temperate] actions, but one who also does them in the way in which just or temperate people do them."

Our discomfort with the language of imitation is but an indication of how distant our understanding of the character of the moral life is—not only from Paul but also from Aristotle. Moreover, once Paul's commen-

107

dation of gentleness, truth, honor, justice, and purity is understood in light of his life, we begin to get a sense that the form these virtues take in those who follow Paul may be quite different than the form they take in those who do not follow Paul. For example, gentleness is not exactly the first characteristic that comes to mind if and when you try to describe the kind of person Paul must have been. Paul, that unrelenting ball of Christ-determined energy, never seems to have backed away from a fight he thought needed to be fought. To be sure, we are to be gentle, but our gentleness must be true—which may require conflict and confrontation.

Thus Paul tells the Philippians to "beware of the dogs, beware of the evil workers, beware of those who mutilate the flesh." To call one's opponents "dogs," even if they are trying to convince gentiles that they can only be followers of Jesus by undergoing circumcision, does not strike us as "gentle." In his letter to the Galatians Paul even wishes that those who would unsettle the Galatians with demands for circumcision "would castrate themselves" (Gal. 5:12). Whatever Paul means by gentleness does not seem to exclude combativeness.

This suggests we need to reconsider our presumption that what it means to be a Christian is not all that different than what most people think it means to be a good person. Note that Paul does not recommend that the Philippians try to be gentle. Rather, he says, "Let your gentleness be known to everyone." They have not become gentle by trying to be gentle, but rather they have been formed into gentleness by being made citizens of heaven, baptized into the death and resurrection of Christ. Such citizenship means that they are a people constituted by the One John the Baptist said was still to come and who Paul was sure had come. There may be some continuity between commonsense morality and Christ-shared virtues, but they are clearly no longer the same thing.

The Paul we are to imitate has been baptized by the fire of the Holy Spirit. Such a baptism means that death and the attempt to live life to avoid death no longer ruled Paul's life. What matters according to Paul is this:

Christ will be exalted now as always in my body, whether by life or death. For to me, living is Christ and dying is gain. If I am to live in the flesh, that means fruitful labor for me; and I do not know what I prefer. I am hard pressed between the two: my desire is to depart and be with Christ, for that is far better; but to remain in the flesh is more necessary for you. Since I am convinced of this, I know that I will remain and continue with all of you for your progress and joy in faith, so that I may share abundantly in your boasting in Christ Jesus when I come to you again. (Phil. 1:20–26)

In our Psalm we are told that we will recognize God's salvation when

> Steadfast love and faithfulness
>   will meet;
>   righteousness and peace will
>   kiss each other.
> Faithfulness will spring up from
>   the ground,
>   and righteousness will look down
>   from the sky.

Yet we know that seldom are truth and mercy in harmony. And it is even less likely for righteousness and peace to correspond. But truth has sprung from the earth—from a cross planted in the earth—because our God emptied himself, taking the form of a slave, humbling himself and becoming obedient to the point of death, even death on a cross. That is the gentleness Paul believes has constituted Christians in the church at Philippi. That is the truthful gentleness Paul commends. For it is surely the case that gentleness abstracted from the truth of the cross becomes but sentimentality, ready to compromise with the worst injustice in the name of a peace that too often only names an order built on violence.

Truth, honor, justice, and purity were, in the ancient world as they are in our world, virtues shaped by a different politics than the politics Paul represented. For pagans the virtues were shaped by heroic lives that exemplified the presumption that death could be defeated by renown. But those heroic stories are not what shapes Paul's understanding of truth, honor, justice, and purity. Paul's politics is an order determined by the Lord who obediently died a cross-determined death. And so Paul is able to exemplify these virtues as a man in jail overwhelmed by his love of Christ.

It is the story of Christ that determines our knowledge of truth, honor, justice, and purity. Truth is known in the silence that refuses to accept Rome's power in the person of Pilate; honor is revealed in the humiliation of the cross; justice is found in the refusal to abandon the least of these; and purity is manifest in the joy of Christ's resurrection, making possible singleness of heart. Paul commends these virtues, confident that the Lord is near, making it possible for the Philippians—and for us—to live in peace, to rejoice, and even to be at rest in a world that knows no peace, joy, or rest.

Gentleness is the form our waiting, our peace, takes. Advent names not simply the season before Christmas but a feature of Christian existence made possible by the nearness of Christ. We believe, as we heard in Zephaniah, that in truth the Lord is in our midst, a gentle warrior who has given us the victory. We believe, moreover, that victory is manifest in this meal of the new age that overturns what the world understands as truth, honor, justice, and purity. For through the transformation constituted by this meal the lame and the outcasts who were shamed by the world have become God's chosen. Once we were no people but now we are a people capable of taking the time, in a world that thinks it has no time, to do, in the words of Jean Vanier, "ordinary things with tenderness."

So my brothers and sisters, "do not worry about anything, but in prayer and supplication with thanksgiving let your requests be known to God. And the peace of God, which surpasses all understanding will guard your hearts and minds in Christ." So formed by the virtues of gentleness, truthfulness, honor, justice, and purity, do not be surprised if you discover that by coming to this table you are not just another good person. You are a Christian. Praise God.

Part IV

EVENTS

14

A Deadly Business

A Sermon for the Baptism of Sierra Rayne Mathewson and Jonas Elliott Church
March 4, 2007

Genesis 15:1–12, 17–18
Psalm 27
Philippians 3:17–4:1
Luke 13:22–35

We live in a death-denying world. Many strive to produce and reproduce a world without death and in doing so appear to desperately love life. But the life they love is determined by death, because for them to live and love requires that they attempt to ensure that they, as well as those they love, will never die. Accordingly, love is driven by fear, governed as it must be by the desperate desire to protect those we love from the reality of death. As a result, life itself becomes a living fatality, just one damn thing after another, so that when death actually comes nothing is lost.

Those who attempt to live life as though they will never die reflect and sustain a correlative politics. The longing to live lives free of death makes those who would so live dependent on and subject to those who claim they can make them safe. Lives lived as if we will not die, lives that aim to take death hostage, are given over to deathly powers so the illusion that people can avoid death is protected. Such powers are omnivorous because they must scour the world to procure the resources necessary to sustain the pretension that they can get out of life alive.

Therefore, what we do today to Sierra and Jonas cannot help but put them in danger.[1] For today they will be given life not only through death but through a particular death. The life they are given through this death is one that threatens those who are hard at work creating a world without death. Baptism is deadly business. To be baptized is to die in Christ and to be raised with him. Through baptism into the life and resurrection of Jesus, Sierra and Jonas are made participants in a living body that defies the culture of death.

That we baptize children, as we will do today, understandably makes us hesitant to call attention to the death-dealing character of baptism. However, when we ignore that baptism entails a death, sentimentality threatens to overwhelm what is done in baptism. Thus the widespread perception that baptism is a rite of initiation to welcome new life into the world. But if this is just a rite of initiation, why do we pray, "We thank you, Father, for the water of Baptism. In it we are buried with Christ in his death"?

Paul makes the deadly character of baptism unmistakably clear in his letter to the church at Rome:

> Do you not know that all of us who have been baptized into Christ Jesus were baptized into his death? Therefore we have been buried with him by baptism into death, so that, just as Christ was raised from the dead by the glory of the Father, so we too might walk in the newness of life.
>
> For if we have been united with him in a death like his, we will certainly be united with him in a resurrection like his. We know that our old self was crucified with him so that the body of sin might be destroyed, and we might no longer be enslaved to sin. For whoever has died is freed from sin. But if we have died with Christ, we believe that we will also live

with him. We know that Christ, being raised from the dead, will never die again; death no longer has dominion over him. The death he died, he died to sin, once and for all; but the life he lives, he lives to God. So you also must consider yourselves dead to sin and alive to God in Christ Jesus. (Rom. 6:3–11)

That we have been united with him in a resurrection life is surely good news, but it is also the case that we have been united with him in a death like his. Indeed it seems we must be so united with him in death if sin is no longer to have power over us. If we say, as we rightly do, "It is not I that live, but Christ," we must also say, "It is not I that die, but Christ." Which means, as Robert Jenson suggests, what we have to do to think of our deaths is to abandon the first person and instead address the risen Son in the second person, thanking him for dying our death.

The death Sierra and Jonas undergo and the life they are given is, therefore, a very specific death and life. Through baptism the baptized have inscribed on their hearts the story of Israel, Jesus, and the church. Their bodies will be storied by the story begun with Abraham, who did not ask God for a life without death. He wanted to know what God would give him, and God gave him an heir and a land. We believe that God kept his promise to Abraham; Jesus is the heir and his body is our land.

Notice how the body is treated in baptism. Our bodies are touched so that through touch we can be incorporated into the ecclesial body of Christ. The bodies of adults and children alike are handled in a manner that makes clear that our bodies are no longer our own. We now belong to Christ and his church. Our bodies are not our possession. Through baptism we are relieved of the power to determine how we will live or how we will die. Now our citizenship is in heaven, which means, according to Paul, that our bodies will be transformed into the body of his glory.

That our citizenship is in heaven creates a counter politics to the politics determined by the denial of death. The Didache puts the matter in stark contrast. According to this ancient church document, baptism separates a way of life from a way of death. The way of life is one determined by the love of God and the love of neighbor. Those who follow the way of life are known by their willingness to bless those who would curse them, pray for their enemies, and fast for those who persecute them—all forms of life that require they learn to live without protection. By contrast, those captured by the way of death are filled with evil desires, guile, malice, arrogance, envy, and pride. They are so possessed because they do not acknowledge their Creator and therefore hate the truth, love lies and vanity, and pursue gain without pity for the poor.

That the Didache identifies the way of life with love is surely right. To be baptized into the death and resurrection of Jesus is to be given the time, in a world that thinks it has run out of time, to love. In Wendell Berry's novel *Andy Catlett: Early Travels*, Andy Catlett reflects that he, who once had grandparents and parents, now has children and grandchildren. He then observes:

> Like the flowing river that is yet always present, time that is always going is always coming. And time that is told by death and birth is held and redeemed by love, which is always present. Time, then, is told by love's losses, and by the coming of love, and by love continuing in gratitude for what is lost. It is folded and enfolded and unfolded forever and ever, the love by which the dead are alive and the unborn welcomed by the womb. The great question of the old and dying, I think, is not if they have loved and been loved enough, but if they have been grateful enough for love received and given, however much. No one who has gratitude is the loneliest one. Let us pray to be grateful to the last.

To be baptized is to be made a citizen of a kingdom of gratitude. But this gratitude does not require that we deny the impact death might have on our lives. Rather, gratitude in this kingdom is the shared realization that death does not mean the end because through Christ we've been given the gift of one another. Gratitude is the fruit of our love of one another made possible through Christ's death and resurrection. Indeed, the only way to experience gratitude without denying the reality of death—whether by endless attempts to avoid it or by refusing to acknowledge it as part of life that rightly incites mourning—is to recognize that the love that constitutes the everyday is possible because Christ first loved us.

The question of whether Sierra and Jonas understand what is being done to them in the baptism is beside the point. How could any of us know what we are doing when we are baptized into the death and resurrection of Jesus? What we do, what the Holy Spirit does through us, in baptism is to make these children a part of a people who have been given the gift of life in Christ. Accordingly they will discover they can risk praying for their enemies, they can risk living lives of peace, and they can love one another because death no longer has dominion over them. What we do today will not make Sierra's and Jonas's lives safe, but it will, with God's help, give them lives worth living.

We are baptized only once, but we are called upon to remember our baptism as we participate as witnesses in the baptism of others. In time, we will expect these children to remind us of our baptism as over the years we will remind them of theirs. In time, particularly as we die, we will rely on them to carry on the remembrance of Christ's love for the world that we celebrate through baptism.

15

To Be Made Human

The Baptism of Virginia Dodson Eichelberger
St. Joseph's Episcopal Church
January 13, 2008

Isaiah 42:1–9
Psalm 29
Acts 10:34–43
Matthew 3:13–17

The baptism of Jesus by John, the first event in Jesus's public ministry, draws us ever more deeply into the mystery of the incarnation. At Christmas we celebrate Jesus's conception and birth. In retelling these stories of Christmas the church realized that to remember and tell those stories well we must say that this child is fully divine yet fully human. We call this discovery the doctrine of the incarnation. Incarnation, however, does not describe a status but rather the reality that names the life Jesus had to live that we might be saved. That life is constituted by his obedience to the will of the Father. His obedience is nowhere more manifest than in Jesus's willingness to be baptized by John in the river Jordan.

John's great gift was to be the one capable of identifying Jesus as the long expected messiah. But this recognition entailed a refusal, since John knew he was unworthy to perform the act being asked of him. For the one who calls for repentance and baptizes with water should himself be baptized by the One who has come to baptize with the fire of the Holy Spirit. John was, of course, right that he should not be the one to baptize Jesus. Yet Jesus refuses John refusal. "For now," Jesus says, he must be baptized by John. Jesus must submit to be baptized by John "for now" because it is in this way all righteousness will be fulfilled, that is, through Jesus's obedience. So John does what Jesus asks and in doing so the heavens are opened. The Spirit of God, as promised in Isaiah, descends, dove-like, and alights on Jesus. A voice from heaven declares: "This is my Son, the Beloved, with whom I am well pleased." The Father responds to the obedience of Jesus and John, transforming John's baptism of water and repentance into the fiery baptism of the Spirit.

Jesus's response to John—"Let it be so for now"—sums up, therefore, the form his obedience to the Father must take. "Let it be so for now" anticipates his prayer in the garden, "My Father, if this cannot pass unless I drink it, your will be done." Jesus, the One without sin, submits to John's baptism and by so doing heralds the obedience of his life, which we name "incarnation." We dare not, therefore, miss the significance of this moment in Jesus's ministry. Jesus's unreserved identification with our humanity, a humanity bent by sin, is manifest by his willing obedience to be baptized by John.

Peter, in his great sermon to the gentiles, sums up this extraordinary event, reminding us "how God anointed Jesus of Nazareth with the Holy Spirit and with power; how he went about doing good and healing all who were oppressed by the devil, for God was with him. We are witnesses to all that he did both in Judea and in Jerusalem. They put him to death by hanging him on a tree; but God raised him on the third day and allowed him to appear, not to all people but to us who were chosen by God as witnesses." Jesus's obedience, even to death by crucifixion, makes our participation in his obedience a reality. We have been made "witnesses."

Herbert McCabe, OP, reflecting on the mystery of the incarnation, makes the striking observation that Jesus, not Adam, was the first human being, "the first member of the human race in whom humanity came to fulfillment, the first human being for whom to live was simply to love—for this is what human beings are for." McCabe, of course, is not stating that prior to Jesus no one was a human being. After all, Jesus had a mother. Rather McCabe uses this dramatic claim to remind us that in Christ, just as John the Baptist preached, the kingdom of heaven not only has come near but is present. Baptism is an apocalyptic act signaling the beginning of a new age, the inauguration of the kingdom of God, in which we are quite literally born again through the obedience of this man.

Jesus's obedience, moreover, makes it possible for us to see what the eternal trinitarian life of God looks like when projected on the screen of sinful human history. Jesus's obedience to the Father is how the eternal procession of the Son from the Father appears in history. That Jesus's life was so filled with controversy, so eventful, leading even to his crucifixion, is simply what being human in a sin-determined world looks like. Yet his response to sin, as we are told in Isaiah, was to do the quiet work of justice by opening the eyes of the blind and by freeing prisoners from their dungeons.

According to McCabe, the recognition of Jesus's humanity frees us from the presumption that we need an explanation, a theory, for why Jesus had to die by crucifixion. Jesus was murdered because we fear being loved by the love that created and sustains us. We were created to be in love with God and one another, which means we only discover our true nature through self-giving, self-abandonment, and being at the disposal of others. We cannot live without love yet we are afraid of the destructive and creative power of love because we fear being out of control. Jesus, obedient to the Father, had no fear of being human, of being loved by the Father, and thus at once becomes for us a threat as well as our salvation.

John Howard Yoder echoes McCabe when he observes that the work of Christ is, at its center, found in his obedience. "Christ was exactly what God meant humans to be: in free communion with God, obeying

God and loving others—even his enemies—with God's love." Jesus, the embodiment of perfect love, refuses to force sinners to be what they were meant to be, but instead bears our sins because such is the way of love.

The church, that community of people created through baptism into the life, death, and resurrection of Jesus, is made up of those who, like John, may rightfully fear the invitation to participate in the Son's obedience. But because, through the Holy Spirit, we are made witnesses to the Father's pleasure in the Son, we are enabled, like John and Jesus, to trust in the Father's will. For the same Spirit that came to rest on Jesus stirs these waters, and it is the same Spirit that affirms God's pleasure in our obedience to his divine will. Indeed, the will of God turns out to be love capable of defeating death, and it is these waters that usher us into the reality of God's will inaugurated in Christ's obedience.

Because Jesus was obedient, because Jesus assumed our flesh, because Jesus willingly submitted to John's baptism, we can confidently baptize Virginia Dodson Eichelberger.[1] Through baptism she is made a human being after the likeness of Christ. If that was not so then baptism would be a violent and cruel imposition of a way of life foreign to her. If baptism did not make us participants in the humanity of Christ then baptism would be no more than an esoteric action of a secret society. But the church has no secrets that cannot be shared, and baptism is our most public action. That is so because the very character of baptism challenges any presumption that might tempt Christians arrogantly to think we can separate ourselves from the world. Through baptism we are made participants in the humanity of Christ, which means ours is a shared humanity because Christ took upon himself the whole of human existence. And this is why baptism is the antithesis of cruelty and violence: because through baptism we are made the human beings we were created to be; that is, we are able to love our neighbor as ourselves.

Moreover baptism is the antithesis of violence and secrecy because the love that redeems, the love we see on the cross of Christ, refuses to storm the gates of our sin violently. To be baptized is to be made a participant in God's nonresistant love. Nonviolence is often thought to be a worthy but unrealized ideal. But that cannot be the case because baptism happens. This is what nonviolent love looks like. The sheer joy that comes when we baptize, the wonder that elicits unexpected tears at baptism, is what nonviolent love feels like. To baptize and to be baptized is the Spirit's gift of nonviolent love—that is, what is done to Virginia today is God's salvation.

Today Virginia Dodson Eichelberger is made a Christian—she will soon be a citizen of the kingdom of God. Today Virginia Dodson Eichelberger is made a human being. She will need all the help she can get if she is to grow into her baptism, if she is to become the human being Jesus's humanity makes possible. We know she will need help if she is to grow into her baptism, to lead an obedient life, because we have learned we too need help to so live. But then that is the great good news of the gospel; that is, through Christ we learn to be loved without regret. Today we can confidently baptize Virginia because Jesus became one of us, was baptized by John, lived obediently even to death, and was raised so that we too might live obedient lives of joyful, self-sacrificing love. Virginia, welcome to humanity.

16

Water Is Thicker than Blood

A Sermon for the Marriage of
Jana Bennett and Joel Schickel
May 21, 2005

Jeremiah 31:31–34
Colossians 3:12–17
Matthew 5:1–12

I have read and reread the Beatitudes, but the text we need for this occasion just does not seem to be there. Jesus surely must have forgotten to say, "Blessed are those about to be married for they will be surprised by what God has done to them." But it just does not seem to have occurred to Jesus to include the married among those who are blessed. I am not sure why the married are not included, but it may be that the married seem to choose to be married whereas the poor, those who mourn, the meek, those who hunger and thirst for righteousness, the merciful, the pure in heart, the peacemakers, and the persecuted each name states of life that happen to those who become disciples of Jesus. Which reminds us that the Beatitudes are not recommendations, but descriptions of the kind of people that result, not surprisingly, from the inauguration of the new age begun by Jesus.

Nor do the Beatitudes help us understand the peculiar character of this marriage, that is, a marriage between a philosopher and a theologian.[1] Jesus does not say, "Blessed are the theologians for they shall be humiliated by their pretension to know God." Nor does he say, "Blessed are the philosophers who will never know if they know anything." Moreover, Jesus does not say, "Blessed are the philosopher and theologian when they marry for they will never be able to determine the relation between faith and reason." This is clearly not a marriage made in heaven. This is clearly a marriage made in the university.

Nor are our texts from Jeremiah or Colossians all that useful for aiding our understanding of what Christians do when we marry. The new covenant God promises to make with Israel, a covenant in which the law is written on the hearts of his people, is not the covenant of marriage. Rather, it is the covenant between God and Israel. To be sure, the new covenant is like that between husband and wife, a covenant Israel betrayed, but it is God's faithfulness to Israel that exemplifies fidelity. The fidelity that should be characteristic of marriage is first learned not in marriage but by intimating God's faithfulness to his people.

We believe, moreover, that God's new covenant, the covenant to be written on the heart, is the covenant that is ours in Christ. Thus we are told in Colossians that we are "God's chosen ones" who should be clothed with compassion, kindness, humility, meekness, and patience. But above all we should clothe ourselves with love—a love that binds us, and all that is, in perfect harmony. Given current romantic assumptions about marriage—that marriage is the result of love between two people who will live in perfect harmony with one another—we may be tempted to think this text in Colossians is about marriage.

But I think it is clear that the love recommended by Colossians is not about marriage, but rather about how Christians are to be related to one another in the one body that is Christ. Indeed, I think it is salutary for those inclined to use this text to underwrite the assumption that marriage determines the character of love to remember that Colossians 3:18–19, the text immediately following our text reads: "Wives, be subject to your husbands, as is fitting in the Lord. Husbands, love your wives and never treat them harshly." Thus my claim that Christians are required to love one another not because they are married, but because they are Christians.

Indeed I think it remarkable that Christians are permitted to marry. After all, marriage (particularly in our culture) threatens to destroy the love that constitutes the church. This is not simply because marriages so often go bad, making those who were friends of the couple choose sides. Rather, just to the extent that marriage in modernity represents a desperate attempt to force and forge an intimacy that can rescue us from our loneliness, marriage for many becomes their church. We should not be surprised it does so because marriage becomes the only relationship left in our world that requires us to face the reality of our self-centeredness and pride.

Which is why I think the texts we have been given for this wedding are appropriate even though they are not first and foremost about marriage. We should not be surprised they are not about marriage given Jana's most recent book, *Water Is Thicker Than Blood*. In her book Jana argues that Christians have failed to understand what we do when we marry or do not marry because we have divorced marriage from its theological home in the history of salvation. She suggests that all Christians, through our baptisms, are constituted by the eschatological states of marriage and virginity. Accordingly the family is reconfigured by baptism, which means blood relations are no longer primary, but rather one's relationship to God. Thus Augustine writes:

It is written in the gospel that when a message was brought to Christ that his mother and brothers, that is, his relatives by birth, were waiting outside unable to come nearer because of the crowd, he answered, "Who is my mother?" "Who are my brothers?" And stretching his hands over his disciples, he said, "These are my brothers"; and then, "Whoever does my Father's will, that person is my brother and mother and sister" (Matthew 12:48–50). What was he teaching us other than to value our spiritual family more highly than relationship by birth, and thus what makes people blessed is not being close to upright and holy persons by

125

blood relationship, but being united with them by obeying and imitating their doctrine and way of life.

Such a view of marriage and the family cannot help but challenge and surprise Christian and non-Christian, who alike hold similar assumptions about marriage in our day. After all, Christianity is often sold on the grounds that it is very good for the family. That it is so is because we are acutely aware that marriage and the family are extremely fragile institutions. Marriage has become at once an option, a lifestyle choice, which many assume should make marriage more stable. After all you do not have to marry, so surely if you do marry you must know what you are doing, thus making marriage a joint venture in mutual satisfaction. What could possibly go wrong given such an understanding of marriage? It seems just about everything can go wrong. For it turns out that the love that is assumed to constitute marriage created by choice is transitory and ephemeral. Moreover marriage so constituted finds itself incapable of hospitality to the stranger who often comes in the form of children. Thus children cannot help but challenge marriage in which love is assumed to be constituted by shared selfishness.

But marriage between Christians, shaped as it is by the love learned in the church, cannot help but be an institution of hospitality. Not only are Christians who marry charged to be hospitable to one another through the gift of fidelity, but they discover their marriage depends on the lives of others. For in fact marriage between Christians is hopeless and impossible if the married are not surrounded by those poor in spirit, if they do not learn from those that mourn, if they lack the resources provided by the meek, if they are robbed of those who hunger and thirst for righteousness, if they lack the example of those who are merciful, if they lose all contact with those who are pure in heart, if they have no friends who practice peace, if there are not among us those who are persecuted for righteousness. Moreover, if Christians have not learned to "bear with one another," if we do not forgive one another as the Lord has forgiven us, if we do not admonish one another in all wisdom, if we do not, with gratitude in our hearts, sing psalms, hymns, and spiritual songs to God, then we cannot encourage one another to marry.

That is why Jana's and Joel's desire that we witness their marriage is such a sign of hope. In 1943 Dietrich Bonhoeffer wrote a wedding sermon for his friends, Eberhard and Renate Bethge, from Tegel prison. He began by observing that "it is right and proper for a bride and bridegroom to welcome and celebrate their wedding day with a unique sense of triumph." He did so, I think, because he rightly saw that by their marriage Eberhard and Renate Bethge refused to let the darkness called Hitler, as well as Hitler's war, overwhelm hope. Bonhoeffer's own engagement as well as the marriage of the Bethges witnessed to his conviction that the people of God, those named in the Beatitudes, by God's good grace exist.

We do not live in times as dark as Bonhoeffer's time, but terror and war do reign in our time. Indeed the terror is all the more terrifying, hidden as it is in the normal. That is why this marriage is such a sign of hope. That is why this marriage is gospel. That is why on this day Jana and Joel become for us our priests making Christ present to us. For by their marriage, an unlikely marriage between a theologian and a philosopher, they proclaim that the kingdom is here aborning, that the blessed exist, making possible their marriage in a world as dark and hopeless as our world seems to be. What extraordinary good news. So bless you, Joel and Jana, for the gift of your marriage.

17

Anointing Grace

A Sermon Celebrating the Ordination
of Grace Hackney
June 18, 2006

1 Samuel 15:34–16:13
Psalm 20
2 Corinthians 5:6–17
Mark 4:26–34

You almost have to think someone set this up. Maybe even God did it. On the Sunday after Grace's ordination the lectionary reading for the day is the story of Samuel's anointing of David to be king of Israel. I wonder if I even need to preach this sermon. You already know how it will or should go. Grace was out tending the sheep, or at least raising her family, but God sent a Samuel, who took the form of a church called Aldersgate United Methodist Church, to discern who among their number would be called into the ministry. Aldersgate had many attractive candidates, but God's choice fell not on a powerful male but on this woman.[1] Is God great or what?

I hope to unsettle this way of reading the text, however, by attending to the details of the story. I do so because I think once we appreciate the ambiguity surrounding what it meant for David to be made king of Israel, we will better understand the significance of Grace's ordination. Samuel had previously anointed Saul to be king of Israel. He had done so because the people of Israel insisted that they have a king so that they "may be like other nations, and that our king may govern us and go out before us and fight battles" (1 Sam. 8:20). Yet just to the extent that Saul acted like other kings, the Lord, who had not been happy with the very idea that Israel should have a king, was sorry that he had made Saul king over Israel. Accordingly the Lord sent Samuel, who grieved over Saul, with the task of choosing from the sons of Jesse, the Bethlehemite, a new king for Israel.

The only problem was that Saul was still alive. Samuel, who is not without political insight, knows anointing a new king while the old king is still alive is risky business. Accordingly he points out to the Lord that if Saul hears what he has done he will surely kill him. So the Lord tells Samuel to go to Bethlehem with a heifer so that he can say he has come to make a sacrifice. This proves to be an important strategy, because the elders of Bethlehem come trembling before Samuel fearing his very presence may make them complicit in a political insurrection. Yet Samuel assures them he comes in peace, desiring to do nothing more than sacrifice to the Lord.

Following the Lord's instructions, Samuel invites Jesse and his sons to attend the sacrifice. One by one each son passes before Samuel. Samuel assumes that the Lord would have him anoint as king the oldest or the most physically impressive. The Lord reminds Samuel, however, that he does not see as mortals see, but rather he looks into the heart. So after seeing and rejecting each of Jesse's seven sons, David, the youngest son, is called from keeping the sheep only to be anointed king of Israel in the presence of his brothers. We are told that from that day forward the spirit of the Lord came mightily upon David. And, as we say, the rest is history.

We love this wonderful and captivating story because we so identify with David. David, the lesser son of a lesser tribe and family, is chosen to be king of Israel. We cannot help but read the story of David's ordination as king in terms of the American story of the underdog's triumph. That is the way, moreover, we would like to think about the ordination of Grace. Grace, a woman with a family, overcame the odds and has now been ordained to the Methodist ministry. Ordination may not be quite as good as being made a king, but it still makes a very good story.

But before we let our fantasies shape our reading of this story, notice that Samuel never does what he says he has come to do—that is, he never sacrifices the heifer. We probably think that is to the good. Animal sacrifice does not seem like a good idea to most of us. Indeed, the very idea of sacrifice is not all that appealing. In general we avoid the language of sacrifice except, perhaps, in reference to those who have died in war. But if we are to appreciate the significance of Samuel's anointing of David we need to understand the significance of sacrifice for Israel.

Sacrifice was God's gift to Israel and necessary for its formation as a holy people, that is, a people capable of witnessing among the nations to the God who had called Israel from Egypt and given her the law. Through the sacrifices of the law Israel was given the means to repent of her sins and, thereby, the ability to approach God through Sabbath. Just as the animal being sacrificed was transformed through fire into smoke in order to reach God, so Israel as a nation was made holy through sacrifice. Thus before Samuel could make the sacrifice he told the elders of Bethlehem to sanctify themselves so that they might be made holy. We are told Samuel also sanctified Jesse and his sons, yet we have no report in the story of David's anointing that Samuel sacrificed the heifer.

I think there is no report of a sacrificed heifer because David will turn out to be the one sacrificed. I realize this seems odd. We assume becoming king means being put in a place in which you sacrifice others but not yourself—or if you sacrifice yourself it's the "I have no free time because there are so many royal banquets" kind of sacrifice. But becoming the king of Israel entailed a kingship different from the ruling powers of other nations. Indeed the king of Israel was obligated to oversee not only Israel's obedience to the law of sacrifice but also Israel's obedience to her one, true sovereign—the Lord. To be king of Israel

130

meant that you must sacrifice all forms of kingship that would direct attention from Israel's true king.

Our Psalm for this morning makes clear the challenge before David. Kings will always have a "day of trouble" in which they will be tempted to take pride in chariots and in horses, but the pride of the one who would be king of Israel will be "in the name of the Lord our God." God will not save Israel with armies; rather, the king of Israel must trust that help will come from the sacrifices made in the sanctuary of the Lord. The office of king in Israel is, therefore, also a priestly office because the king must rule sacrificially and Israel might learn to live because of his sacrifice.

David's sad life is a testimony to how difficult it was to be the priest/king of Israel. David's rule is ample evidence that he, like Saul, found it difficult not to imitate kings who had learned to trust in chariots and horses. Indeed David's unfaithfulness meant that he was forbidden to build the temple in which the sacrifice necessary to atone for his and Israel's sin might be performed. David, indeed the kingship itself, was sacrificed that Israel might learn how to be God's sacrifice for the world.

We believe, however, Israel's desire to have a king was fulfilled. Jesus, the new David, a king who was without sin, has been sacrificed that the world might know that all sacrifice has been brought to an end. Through his crucifixion and resurrection Jesus has made it possible for a people to exist who desire no king but the crucified one. Such a people, moreover, learn to survive through the gifts of humility and holiness found in the sharing of the body and blood of Christ.

Grace can, therefore, be ordained because of the work of Christ; his sacrifice requires that no further sacrifice be made. Accordingly Grace has been set aside by the laying on of hands to do for the church what only the whole church can do. She has been given the power to be for us Christ by presiding at the meal in which we become participants in Christ's sacrifice. Grace has been ordained to represent for us Christ's priesthood, through which we are made participants and witnesses to his sacrifice. Yet she will be tempted, and we will tempt her, to use her priesthood to make us safe, to make us a people like other people,

rather than to learn to live trusting only in the one who is our crucified king.

We, like Israel, are tempted to confuse her office with those of other
nations. For example, it is tempting to think Grace has been ordained
because every community needs "leaders." But if we have ordained
Grace to be a "leader" then we are no better than the people of Israel,
who desired a king in order to be like other nations. Grace has not been
ordained to be a leader. Grace has been ordained to be for us a priest
representing Christ's priesthood. Whatever leadership she gives must
be determined by that priestly office.

While the church needs the power God has bestowed on Grace
through her ordination, we will also be tempted to fear and distrust her
because of the power she has been given. As our priest we will expect
and want her to be present with us during times of great pain, suffering,
and vulnerability. Because we so desperately need her at those times
we will also fear her because she will have seen us when our lives are
unguarded and exposed. Any minister will tell you that often those
who have called on them during a crisis will, if possible, avoid having
any relation with the minister after the crisis is over. Indeed, some will
even turn on the one who has been present to them, seeking to restore
the power they fear they have lost.

Because Grace knows her ordination can lead us to fear and distrust
her, she will be tempted to feign humility by assuring us she is the same
"old Grace." But she is not the same. She is now a priest, God's anointed,
to be for us what the church has been called to be for the whole world.
Therefore we can no longer regard her from a human point of view,
because, as Paul reminds us, "if anyone is in Christ, there is a new
creation." That new creation we believe to be bestowed on us through
baptism. And that baptism, in which we are united with Christ in his
death and resurrection, is the only basis we have for our belief that the
power that has been bestowed on Grace will sanctify and strengthen
her and the church she serves.

Yet learning to see and live as the community of the "new creation"
is not easily done. We will need all the help we can get. Jesus taught in
parables to help us see the "new" in creation, that is, to help us see that

the world is charged with the glory of God's redemption. The name of that redemption is the kingdom of God. And that kingdom Jesus compares to seed scattered on the ground that suddenly and surprisingly appears. Or the kingdom is like a mustard seed, the smallest of all seeds, yet it grows to become the greatest of all shrubs. In short, if we are to learn to be a community in which Grace's priesthood reflects for us our great high priest who is Christ, we must learn to live by surprise—which is but another name for the miracle called Eucharist.

In the Eucharist the miraculous life and ministry of the church—a ministry to which Grace has now been called—is revealed. For the Eucharist is the miracle of God's kingdom interrupting time. As a Eucharistic community we participate in this interruption by doing things as ordinary as planting a garden. As a church you have planted a garden. What a strange thing for a church to do. In the midst of a war, in the midst of a world suffering from hunger, you plant a garden to share food with whoever needs it in this place. What a useless gesture. But it is exactly through such gestures that Christ's kingdom is manifest.

Grace, time and time again, will enact Christ's priesthood by presiding at his Eucharist. By doing so she will be a reminder that we have but one true priestly king—Christ the Lord. Therefore, we rightly rejoice in her ordination, because we know it to be God's gift to her and to us so that we might be made holy: For it turns out that holiness is but a name for a people who are not afraid to live by surprise.

Appendix

Matthew
Making the Familiar Strange

Matthew again?[1] I suspect that is an irrepressible thought for many confronted by the return to the Gospel of Matthew in the lectionary cycle. Matthew again—same old familiar texts that will challenge those obligated to follow the lectionary to find something new to say to a congregation that has heard them try to find something new too many times. The result, I fear, too often means that preachers focus their sermons, not on Matthew, but on anecdotes about their life or life in general.

I am quite sympathetic with those who find themselves thinking, *Matthew again?* I confess I found myself in a similar position when asked to write a commentary of the Gospel of Matthew for the new commentary series published by Brazos Press. Under the general editorship of Professor Rusty Reno of Creighton University, this series is committed to recovering a theological reading of Scripture. Accordingly, many theologians are being asked to do what they seldom do, that is, write a commentary on a book of the Bible. I was given Matthew.

In preparation for that task I read commentary after commentary on Matthew. I read ancient as well as modern commentaries, and in the process I learned a great deal. Confronted by my sense of inadequacy to comment on God's Word, I was tempted to rely on the familiar by reporting what I had learned from others. God knows I did not want to get caught with my scholarly pants down. But then, the point of the Brazos project is to put theologians in a position that makes it impossible for them to avoid the Bible. In short, the project is meant to force us to rediscover what Karl Barth described as the "strange new world of the Bible."

It would be presumptuous for me to claim I was able to make the familiar strange, but I can report that having been forced to read Matthew theologically, I discovered a new world. That is exactly what we are meant to discover if I am right that Matthew is the story of the new creation. Matthew begins, "The book of the genesis of Jesus Christ," which, I suggest at the beginning of my commentary, is a modest beginning. The Gospel of Matthew, like the Gospel of John, begins with the extraordinary claim that Jesus is the One who "in the beginning was the Word." In Jesus we see the end that was the beginning.

Suddenly the familiar had become strange. Creations, after all, are not everyday affairs. The word we use to describe this challenge to all that we know is "apocalyptic." The Gospel of Matthew is meant to train us to see the world anew by drawing us into the kingdom of God through learning to become disciples of this man, this messiah, named Jesus. So our task is not to make the Gospel intelligible in light of the world we live in. Rather, our task is to allow the text to reveal how the world we live in has been transformed through this agent of the new creation.

In the words of David Hart, the Gospel of Matthew is meant to teach us to see two realities at once,

> one world (as it were) within another; one the world we know in all its beauty and terror, grandeur and dreariness, delight and anguish, and the other world in its first and ultimate truth, not simply "nature" but "creation," an endless sea of glory, radiant with the beauty of God in every part, innocent of all violence. To see in this way is to rejoice and mourn at once, to regard the world as a mirror of infinite beauty, but as

glimpsed through the veil of death; it is to see the creation in chains, but beautiful as in the beginning of days.

Asking *Matthew again?* betrays the presumption that we need to make an ancient text meaningful to a people who on the whole find the Bible unintelligible. We are too familiar with the story, for example, of the birth of Jesus to recognize how that story is meant to turn our world upside down. But approach that story with the recognition that this One born of Mary is the Second Person of the Trinity, and I think you will find that familiar story makes the world strange. Preaching the nativity becomes proclamation of a new time that challenges our very presumption that we know what time is. Our task is not to make the virgin birth intelligible but to show why our world is unintelligible if Jesus was not born of Mary, the virgin Mother of God.

Good God, does this mean I believe that perhaps the Gospel of Matthew is the revelation of God? By following Jesus to Jerusalem and the cross are we privileged to be drawn up into the very life of God? This is exactly what I think, or at least it is from that perspective I tried to read and write with Matthew. Therefore, when Jesus asks that "this cup pass from me," he is not asking that he be able to escape death. Rather, the cup from which he asks to be relieved is a separation from the Father that only he can undergo. Here in this moment of agony we are witnesses to the intensity of the love that constitutes the life of the Trinity. It is the same love that moves the sun and the stars. It is a love that creates.

If I learned anything from trying to write a theological commentary on the Gospel of Matthew it is a respect for the sheer inexhaustibility of the text. Which means reading Matthew again is not a burden, but a great opportunity. After two thousand years we have only begun to scratch the surface of what it might mean to be a people of the new creation. We need to return again and again to the training Matthew means to subject us to so that we might learn to see the world as created and redeemed by Jesus of Nazareth. *Matthew again?*—thank God!

Preaching Repentance
in a Time of War

Dear God, we are in a mess.[2] By "we" I mean Christians in America. I believe we are in a mess because as Christians in America we are more American than Christian. That we are more American than Christian was clearly indicated by the Christian response to September 11, 2001. Christians assumed that the "we" in "we are at war" was the Christian "we." I will suggest that our identification of the Christian "we" with the American "we" should, at the very least, give Christians pause. Put even more forcefully, as a people called to repentance we must discern what repentance might mean if we are to distinguish the Christian "we" from the American "we." I do not pretend that such discernment is a simple matter.

Some may think that Americans losing confidence in the war in Iraq is a sign that we may be ready to rethink our response to September 11, 2001. Americans are finally coming to our senses. I am not sure how to read the American dis-ease with the war, but I fear that the unwillingness to support the war has more to do with the inability to "win" than with any profound moral reassessment of the presuppositions that seemed to legitimize the war in the first place.

After all, most Americans, Christian or non-Christian, were enthusiastic about the war in its early stages. Even if there were no weapons of mass destruction, the war was assumed to be justified because it was part of the "War on Terrorism." That no clear relation between Saddam Hussein and Osama Bin Laden, aside from their being "bad" men, could be established was thought by most to be an insignificant detail. Perhaps even more troubling than the general American approval of the war was the assumption that a war on terrorism made sense or could be justified.

Lent is an appropriate time to try to fathom how we got in the mess we are in. After all, Lent is the time the church has set aside for the examination of conscience in the hope that we might identify and repent of our sins. Yet it is by no means clear what it might mean to preach repentance at this time in our country. Who is the "we" that is to do the repenting? Do we really expect "the nation" to be capable of repentance? What sin can be named from which we should repent? How can a "prophetic call to repent" avoid the sin of self-righteousness?

Moreover the political challenge for the preacher who would preach on repentance in a time of war, even during Lent, is not easily negotiated. How could anyone preach about the war in Iraq without seeming to "take a side" politically? Even those American politicians who are critics of the war are required to make clear that, though they are critical of the war, they are unwavering in support of our soldiers, who are doing their duty. Try suggesting in a sermon that Christians who find themselves in the military may not have adequately examined their conscience as Christians, and you will discover that there are very definite limits to preaching repentance.

Please note that I am not suggesting that those in the military are implicated in sin in a manner that those who are not in the military are not. Most Christians in the military have never had it suggested to them that Christians have or should have a problem with war. In fact most Christians, at least most American Christians, do not believe that Christians have a problem with war. They may well think war is "not a good thing," but they also believe that sometimes war is necessary. It simply does not occur to them that their assumption that war is not a problem for Christians may be an indication that sin has us under possession. Indeed that way of putting the matter is profoundly offensive to most American Christians, who sinfully think that sin is something we do rather than a power that possesses us.

I suspect these kinds of challenges are why most of the sermons on repentance during Lent concentrate on "personal" confession of sin and repentance. We, and by "we" I mean most American Christians, are simply incapable of confessing sin as a community. As a result, our understanding of sin tends to be "moralistic." We think of sin as some particular "bad habit" that if we try hard enough we can break. We even believe our guilt can be trusted to indicate what our sins may be, thus failing to recognize that our guilt too often is but the form our unfailing narcissism takes.

I certainly do not want to deny the significance of individual self-examination or repentance. I do, however, have deep reservations regarding whether or not we are even capable of knowing on our own what our sins may be. That we think repentance is primarily about "my sin" makes it extremely difficult to make sense of what it might mean to confess our sin as a people. Yet interestingly enough, most of the Scripture we read during Lent directs our attention not to "my" sins but to our sins. The church can hardly expect a nation to be able to confess its sin as a nation unless the church is capable of expressing our common sin as a church. And I do not think that we can learn to preach repentance as a church without the practice of penance.

I am a communicant of the Church of the Holy Family (Episcopal) in Chapel Hill, North Carolina. It is typical for us to use the Penitential Order to begin the liturgy during Advent and Lent at Holy Family. After the commencement of the "war against terrorism," however, all liturgies, except those during Christmas and Easter, at the Church of the Holy Family begin with the Penitential Rite. By beginning our worship in this way I believe we are learning what it might mean to repent as a people during the time of war.

The use of the Penitential Rite to begin the liturgies at Holy Family after September 11, 2001, was accompanied by an explanatory paragraph in our bulletin. The paragraph reads: "*The Penitential Order*: During these Sundays after Pentecost while the United States and its allies are at war in Iraq and Afghanistan, we begin our celebrations of the Holy Eucharist with the Penitential Order, mindful for repentance and praying for the life of the world." This paragraph makes it unmistakably clear that our penitential practice is directly related to living in a country at war.

The phrasing of the paragraph is extremely important. For example, when we first implemented the practice of beginning our liturgies with the Penitential Rite, the paragraph in the bulletin began this way, "During the time when we are at war in Iraq and Afghanistan, we begin our celebrations of the Holy Eucharist with the Penitential Order, mindful for repentance and praying for the life of the world." Several members of the church, however, objected to that way of putting the matter because the "we" suggested that the church and America were the same. They did not deny that the identification of the American "we" and the Christian "we" may be descriptively accurate, but they did not want the description to become a normative presumption. They worried that the grammar of the "we" in the phrase "we are at war" might suggest that the church cannot be distinguished from the nation.

This may well seem a small matter, but I think it a crucial distinction if we are to sustain the penitential discipline of the church. For the church is able to repent because the church is able to recognize sin in a manner that the American "we" cannot. The current wording in the bulletin does not deny that Christians in America are implicated in the war, but the wording, "the United States and its allies are at war," is an acknowledgment that Christians, if we are to be a witness against ourselves, must be a people who are able to be distinguished from America. It is the United States and its allies who are at war, not the church or Christians.

Yet the wording also makes clear that as Christians in America we cannot divorce ourselves from America. That America is at war no doubt reflects our failure as Christians to help others understand why we have a problem with war. Because we have been given the gift of God's peace, the same peace we share with one another before we receive the body and blood of Christ, we know we are called to be an alternative to the world's presumption that there is no alternative to war. So the wording of the announcement in the bulletin is important to enable us as Christians to name our sins as well as be of service to the society in which we find ourselves.

But equally important is the Penitential Order itself. The Order begins by our being addressed by the celebrant in the name of the Father, Son, and Holy Spirit. We are confronted with the Decalogue by being directed to "hear the commandments of God to his people: I am the Lord your God who brought you out of bondage. You shall have no other gods but me." We are instructed to respond, "Amen. Lord, have mercy." We are, therefore, not addressed as individuals but as a people who must confess our sins as a people.

After the great commandment is read we are then invited to confess our sins before God and our neighbor using this prayer:

> Most merciful God,
> We confess that we have sinned against you
> In thought, word, and deed,
> By what we have done,
> And by what we have left undone.
> We have not loved you with our whole heart;
> We have not loved our neighbors as ourselves.
> We are truly sorry and we humbly repent.
> For the sake of your Son Jesus Christ,
> Have mercy on us and forgive us;
> that we may delight in your will,
> and walk in your ways,
> to the glory of your Name. Amen.

The grammar of the confession therefore makes it impossible for us to try to take possession of our sins as though our sins do not implicate the whole body. That is why the celebrant declares us forgiven saying: "Almighty God have mercy on you, forgive you all your sins through our Lord Jesus Christ, strengthen you in all goodness, and by the Holy Spirit keep you in eternal life." Our confession of sin is a confession of a people, and the forgiveness offered is the forgiveness of a people.

By having our sins identified by the Decalogue we undergo training to name our sins in the hope that we might begin to see, for example, that there is a connection between learning not to lie, not taking God's name in vain, and our willingness to kill. For if the church does not simply provide an alternative to war but is an alternative to war she must help those who worship God discover that our violence lies in our failure to live the truth that comes through the body and blood of Christ.

But how does this help us preach repentance in time of war? At the very least it invites those obligated to preach the Word of God to make connections otherwise impossible. Killing in war may be an indication of the power sin has over our lives, but to "preach against war," to preach against the war in Iraq, can be an empty gesture. "Prophetic preaching" may win plaudits for the preacher for being courageous, but it does little to help us locate what it might mean to repent. We must begin by asking: what are the practices that have led the church in America to forget that Christians have or should have a problem with war?

For the reason Christians have a problem with war draws on our most fundamental action; that is, through the Eucharist we have been "accepted as living members of Jesus Christ" and thus sent into the world in peace. Word and sacrament cannot be separated, lest we be tempted to forget that the church is God's alternative to war. This is what makes it possible to preach repentance in a manner that avoids the impression that one is choosing sides in the current arena of American politics. But this also means that preaching repentance in a time of war is possible only if the preaching prior to the time of war has been determined by the "politics of God."

The name of the "politics of God" is church. Preaching is a gift given to the church to aid those who worship God in making the connections necessary to see the world truthfully. Thus my claim that the first task of the church is not to make the world more just, but to make the world the world. For the world cannot know it is the world unless a people exist who are called from the world to be an alternative to the world. How can the world know there is an alternative to war unless a people exist who, shaped by the Word of God, know they are not to kill—even in war?

I am well aware that to preach repentance for the Christian support of war seems a daunting task given the situation of mainline Protestant churches in America. Those who make up the mainline churches of America do not believe that the church is an alternative to war. They do not believe the church is an alternative to war because they have never heard sermons that suggest that the church is an alternative to war. Rather, most of the sermons they hear offer little more than "insights" into the human condition. Judgment and repentance is left to the fundamentalists, who are happily despised because they are judgmental. The problem with the fundamentalists, however, is not that they are judgmental or that they call for repentance, but rather the problem is that what they assume to be under judgment reflects presumptions of the well-off American middle class rather than a people determined by the Decalogue.

So if we are to preach repentance during a time of war we must, as those who preach, begin by repenting of how we have failed to preach truthfully. Let us say to our congregations that we feared their reactions if we had preached that Christians have a problem with war. But we now repent of our cowardice and, at the very least, that means we must learn the difference that being Christian, even in America, makes. Preach that and I promise you will have a very memorable Lent.

Connecting Some of the Dots, or
An Attempt to Understand Myself

I have always been resistant to providing any overall account of my work. Indeed I am not even happy with the idea of "my work." I have never wanted to claim what I do as a possession. Of course the refusal to take responsibility for what one has done can be irresponsible, but I worry that ownership language may betray what I take to be the communal character of the theological enterprise. As I understand it, theology is in service to the church, which means it is best done in a conversational and non-system-building manner. Perhaps another way to put the matter is that I do not want—and I hope I do not have—a position. Barth observed that "the great temptation and danger consists in this, that the theologian will actually become what he seems to be—a philosopher." When theology mimics philosophy, or at least philosophy after Kant and Hegel, you have an indication that the theologian may be unable to resist the prideful attempt to make theology something more than a servant. In modernity it has been very hard for theologians to resist the presumption that their task is to provide more determinative accounts of the truth of what Christians believe, accounts that are more basic than the beliefs themselves. Thus my observation: if you think you need a theory of truth to underwrite the conviction that Jesus was raised from the dead, then worship that theory—not Jesus.

This is simply another way of saying that my reasons for being a non-foundationalist have always been theological. Indeed, I have never been happy with the foundationalist/non-foundationalist alternatives. Those alternatives unfortunately reproduce the epistemological presumptions of modernity, that is, that you need a theory of knowledge in order to know what you know. Such a view seems to me fundamentally mistaken just to the extent it produces and reproduces the ahistorical liberal subject. I have obviously been deeply shaped by MacIntyre's tradition-determined account of rationality exactly because MacIntyre rightly helps us see that the epistemological turn in philosophy was a mistake.

Accordingly, I have understood my task to be little more than an attempt to assemble reminders about how Christian convictions work when the work they should do is in good order. I am identified with (1) the recovery of the importance of the virtues for understanding the Christian life, (2) an emphasis on narrative for the intelligibility of an action description, (3) a correlative emphasis on the significance of the church as a community necessary for the formation of people of virtue, (4) criticism of the accommodation of the church to liberal political arrangements, and (5) an emphasis on the significance of nonviolence as a hallmark of the Christian way of being in the world. Yet I think none of these emphases, though they are interdependent and interrelated, amount to a position.

I do not believe that theology can be a "system," but I do believe that what the church believes is interconnected. Accordingly the theologian's task is to try to help the church maintain the connections necessary for telling the story of God's creative and redeeming work. Connecting the dots, however, means that the specializations that dominate contemporary theology must be challenged. Specialization has too often had the unhappy effect of separating theology from the practices of the church—practices as basic as prayer. That means I have tried not to think of myself as an "ethicist" or a "moral theologian," but rather I have simply tried to be a theologian. But the way I have done theology is quite frustrating for those intent on maintaining "boxes" to characterize various forms of theology. I am not sufficiently conservative for conservatives nor am I liberal enough for liberals. Labels just do not seem to work to describe what I do.

I appreciate the fact, however, that those unfamiliar with my work find it hard to know where to begin. Moreover, I have written more than anyone should write. But writing is necessary if you think that theology is investigative. I simply cannot "sum it up," but I will try to connect some of the dots that make up the jumble that is my work. Yet I am sure that I am not the best reporter of my work. In a blurb for Samuel Wells's book, *Transforming Fate into Destiny: The Theological Ethics of Stanley Hauerwas*, I noted that "Wells is one of those wonderful readers who understand me better than I understand myself."[3] If you understand the influence of Wittgenstein on me you will understand that this is not my attempt to be self-effacing. I do not believe I have a "mind" that would make me the best interpreter of what I think, because what I think is not mine. Accordingly, I will use Wells's account of "my work" to try to connect the dots.

In *Transforming Fate into Destiny*, Wells suggests an evolution in my work from quandary to character, from character to story, from story to community, from community to church, from space to time, from tragedy to irony, and finally from fate to destiny. I think this is a very interesting genealogy, and my only reservation about it is the word "from." The word "from" can suggest, a suggestion that Wells does not make, that I have left behind character, or narrative, or the stress on community. Rather, what has happened is that these conceptual tools have been rearranged as I have slowly acquired a more determinative theological voice.

Wells is quite right, however, that I begin hoping to challenge the focus on decisions in contemporary ethics by a recovery of the virtues. I did so primarily in the hope of providing a way out of the limited "situation ethics" debate generated by the work of Joseph Fletcher. Aristotle and Aquinas were my primary sources for developing an alternative to situation ethics, which made it all the more surprising for me to discover that moral theology in the Roman Catholic context suffered from some of the same problems associated with the Protestant emphasis on decisions.

What I think some have failed to understand about this early work is the influence of Wittgenstein and Anscombe on my efforts to reframe how ethics was to be understood. For at the heart of my attempt to recover a robust account of the virtues was a correlative understanding of the crucial character of language, and in particular the role of description, for the moral life. I was sure Iris Murdoch was right to say, "You can only act in the world that you can see," but I thought it also the case that "you can only see what you have come to say." So the virtues name the ongoing habits necessary to sustain a life not determined by choice. Thus Murdoch's claim that "choices are what you do when everything else has been lost."

Accordingly I found myself in deep sympathy with the work of Herbert McCabe and, in particular, his account of the nature of ethics in *Law, Love, and Language*.[4] McCabe, drawing on Wittgenstein and Aquinas, rightly challenged the dualism between internal/external, body/soul that bedevils modern modes of thought. As McCabe puts it, "Instead of saying that I have a private mind and a public body, a mind for having concepts in and a body for saying and hearing words, I say I have a body that is able to be with other bodies not merely by physical contact but by linguistic communication. Having a soul is just being able to communicate; having a mind is being able to communicate linguistically. The meaning of a word, then, is the purpose it serves in the communication between people in a certain community."[5]

For Christians that "certain community" is called the church, which McCabe observes "makes the presence of Christ articulate as a language, as an interpretation of the world, as a means of communication." What is to be communicated is that through the resurrection of Jesus the world has been redeemed, has been made different. The "church exists to articulate this difference, to show the world to itself."[6] I should like to think that my work is but a footnote to McCabe's understanding of what it means "to show."

The significance of showing, of calling attention to how, as Christians, we must learn to describe the world, is crucial to understanding how I have tried to reframe moral questions. Rather than asking, "Why is suicide or abortion wrong?" or, "What exceptions might there be, given the prohibition against suicide or abortion?" I asked, "What kind of virtues do we need for these descriptions to be intelligible?" By asking that question, moreover, I was led to ask, "What kind of community do we need for the formation of a people capable of sustaining the habits of speech and corresponding virtues to make the prohibition of suicide and abortion life-giving?" In other words, such prohibitions are only meant to mark boundaries for a people who live in a manner that questions regarding suicide or abortion are not asked.

This led me inexorably to the discovery of the significance of narrative. Descriptions like suicide or abortion are not just "givens," but rather are the achievement of a people who are shaped by narrative-determined practices that make such descriptions part of a complex way of life. For example, I think it is not accidental that Christians in the early church were identified by their unwillingness to kill their children as well as their willingness to offer hospitality to the stranger. I think, moreover, that the prohibition against abortion is but an implication of the church's obligation to welcome the stranger. Accordingly I have tried to show how negative prohibitions are reflections of more determinative positive convictions.

The interrelated themes of virtue, language, descriptions, and narrative increasingly led me to take a critical stance toward the political arrangements associated with liberal social orders. I am quite well aware that there are many "liberalisms," just as there are many "modernities," but it became increasingly apparent to me that liberalism named the project aimed at developing political arrangements without memory. Thus my claim that modernity names the attempt to produce people who believe they should have no story except the story they chose when they had no story. This is called "freedom," and it is assumed such an account of freedom is necessary to sustain an account of morality that cannot acknowledge that we live by gift.

My problem with liberal political arrangements is not that they are liberal, but rather that Christians confuse such arrangements with Christianity. Wells notes that not all of my criticisms of liberal social and political practices depend on specific theological claims. That is true, but when I develop criticisms of liberalism using what I have learned from non-theological sources (Wolin, Coles, Connolly) I do so because I think liberalism is not only bad for Christians but also for liberals.[7] It is so because the self that is formed by liberal practice lacks the substance to be virtuously habituated to acknowledge our character as "dependent rational animals."

For example, the problem with the story that you should have no story except the story you chose when you had no story is that it is false. The power of that story, however, is undeniable. In order to illustrate how the power of the liberal story shapes our lives, I often ask people if they believe they should be held responsible for decisions they made when they did not know what they were doing. The answer is invariably that we should not be held responsible for decisions we made when we did not know what we were doing. I then observe that such a view makes marriage unintelligible. Of course you did not know what you were doing when you promised life-long monogamous marriage, but Christians are going to hold you to promises you made when you did not know what you were doing. That is why Christians demand that marriage be a public act: because you will need witnesses to remind you of your promises.

If marriage is rendered unintelligible by the presumption that I can only be held accountable for decisions I made when I knew what I was doing, then the bringing of children into the world is even more problematic. You will never get the children you thought you wanted. The illusory assumption that you can leads to two perverse postures: (1) the presumption that children must be conceived and born only under the most favorable circumstances, and (2) the presumption that the children we have must be perfect. As a result there is little joy in the having of children in our day and, perhaps worse, such a view of children, as Rowan Williams suggests in *Lost Icons*, makes it difficult to sustain an account of childhood because we are no longer sure what it means to be an adult.[8]

I have used this analysis of our "freedom" to suggest that too often the understanding of the moral life in modernity at best mimics stoicism. For we must come to recognize that we have been fated by the story that we should have no story except the story we chose when we had no story. So at best we have to come to terms with the fated-ness of what we did when we thought we knew what we were doing but on reflection must recognize that what we "chose" was as much what happened to us as what we did. I take the great representatives of this kind of stoicism to be Kant and Freud.

Wells nicely puts the matter this way:

> The ethical tradition which Hauerwas in his early years calls "the standard account" is coloured by its implicit perception of fate and destiny: the tragic fate of the individual whose crises of decision are insoluble in conventional terms, and the limited destiny of the rebellion which claims that "love is all you need." Hauerwas finds in the detail of story, particularly through gifted storytellers like Trollope, a display of how a person of character can embody the destiny of their calling amid the givens of their circumstances. Only the Christian story, however, can form a community which treasures, rather than fears, the truth, and can look to its destiny with such hope that it needs no violence to overcome the givens of its existence.[9]

Wells suggests, however, that in my early work I had not taken advantage of the Christian hope determined by the conviction that the Christian story has an end. He argues that the church's and the Christian's confidence that we have a destiny enables the church and the Christian to face the tragedies of life not from a tragic but from an ironic perspective. Such a stance does not depend on a spatial separation from all that might diminish the church's integrity, but rather entails an understanding of time. Wells observes, "Instead of acting to make the world come out right, the church acts according to the eschatological truth it believes about God. Thus it performs everyday, time-consuming tasks, just like the rest of the world: but for different reasons. It therefore appears to be a satire on society."[10]

I should like to think that I have taken to heart Wells's suggestion about time in my latter work. I have done so, however, also under the influence of Yoder's account of nonviolence. For no account of nonviolence can be sustained that does not involve the massive metaphysical claim that we have all the time we need to live nonviolently in a world of violence. Thus my claim that Christians are not called to live nonviolently because we think that nonviolence is a strategy to rid the world of war, but rather, as faithful followers of Christ in a world of war, we believe we have been given all the time we need to live nonviolently. For nonviolence, like the virtues, is necessary if we are to live well as witness to an alternative world called the "kingdom of God."

Christians, of course, do not believe that we can live as if we should have no story except the story we chose when we had no story. We do not believe that story because, as Wells suggests, we believe we are part of an eschatological story that has a beginning, a calling of the people (Israel), the sending of the Son whose name is Jesus, church time, and an end called the eschaton.[11] Accordingly Christians know that they are part of a drama they have not created. Indeed we believe that at the heart of what it means to be a Christian is to learn to be a creature—that is, we do not exist to receive a gift, but our very existence is gift.

This means that Christians cannot help but find themselves in tension with the liberal moral and political projects. For those projects presuppose that we can live as if God does not exist. Which means we cannot avoid the recognition that the God in which Christians believe–that is, the Father, Son, and Holy Spirit—cannot be worshiped without that worship constituting a contrasting politics to the way the world runs. I, therefore, find myself in great sympathy with the encyclical tradition that rightly saw that the primary social challenge of modernity is atheism. For example in *Quadragesimo Anno* we are told:

The root and font of this defection in economic and social life from the Christian law, and of the consequent apostasy of great numbers of workers from the Catholic faith, are the disordered passions of the soul, the sad result of original sin which has so destroyed the wonderful harmony of many faculties that, easily led astray by his evil desires, he is strongly incited to prefer the passing goods of this world to the lasting goods of Heaven. Hence arises that unquenchable thirst for riches and temporal goods, which has at all times impelled men to break God's laws and trample upon the rights of their neighbors but which on account of the present system of economic life, is laying far more numerous snares for human frailty.

A politics based on the irrelevance of God, moreover, cannot help but be a politics that can make no sense of death or suffering. Leo XIII in his encyclical *Laetitiae Sanctae* (September 8, 1893) rightly observed that one of the great evils that besets modern life

> is to be found in repugnance to suffering and eagerness to escape whatever is hard or painful to endure. The greater number are thus robbed of that peace and freedom of mind which remains the reward of those who do what is right undismayed by the perils or troubles to be met with in doing so. Rather do they dream of a chimeric civilization in which all that is unpleasant shall be removed, and all that is pleasant shall be supplied. By this passionate and unbridled desire of living a life of pleasure, the minds of men are weakened, and if they do not entirely succumb, they become demoralized and miserably cower and sink under the hardships of life.

In contrast to such a view of the world, Leo XIII observes that the Christian does not shrink from following in the footsteps of Christ, patiently enduring great things. But such patience is not the empty stoicism of simply enduring pain. It is instead that patience which is learned from the humble example of Jesus. "It is the patience which is learned from the example of Him, who 'having joy set before Him endured the cross, despising the shame' (Heb. 16:2). It is the patience which is obtained by the help of his grace; which shirks not a trial because it is painful, but which accepts it and esteems it as gain, however hard it may be to undergo."

I call attention to this passage from Leo XIII's encyclical because it is the necessary presupposition for understanding my work in medical ethics, as well as my focus on caring for children and, in particular, the mentally disabled. The practice of medicine is morally determined by the presumption that we are not to abandon the sick even if, or when, they cannot be cured. Medicine, in short, draws on the Christian practice of presence. Yet with the modern presumption that suffering of all kinds—and of course there are forms of suffering that we rightly wish to avoid or cure—should be eliminated, the practice of medicine threatens to become the way the sick and disabled are eliminated. By focusing on the care of the mentally handicapped, therefore, I hope to help us see what it means to learn to endure. Such endurance I think is unintelligible if the God we worship as Christians does not exist.

I like to think of this aspect of my work as exemplifying a "natural theology." I am, of course, a Barthian, but in spite of Barth's rejection of natural theology I am convinced Barth thought on an ad hoc basis that Christian and non-Christian alike can have intimations of how we get our lives right as well as how we get our lives wrong. Barth, I think, would have no difficulty agreeing with John Howard Yoder's claim that

> when the "nature of things" is properly defined, the organic relationship to grace is restored. The cross is not a scandal to those who know the world as God sees it, but only to the pagans, who look for what they call wisdom, or the Judeans, who look for what they call power. It has always been true that suffering creates shalom. Motherhood has always meant that. Servanthood has always meant that. Healing has always meant that. Tilling the soil has always meant that. Prophecy has always meant that. What Jesus did—and we might say it with reminiscence of Scholastic Christological categories—was that he renewed the definition of king-ship to fit with the priesthood and prophecy. He saw that the suffering servant is king as much as he is priest and prophet. The cross is neither foolish nor weak, but natural.[12]

What I refuse to do is use the abstraction "nature" to underwrite the attempt to do ethics as if God does not exist. I am particularly critical of those attempts to develop a "natural law ethics" in the interest of sustaining an alleged common morality for liberal social orders. Catholic conservatives and Catholic liberals sometimes have a tendency to distort Aquinas's account of natural law by appealing to natural law abstracted from Aquinas's understanding of the virtues. That is why I find I am so sympathetic to Pinckaers's insistence that

> one needs to remember that the virtues form an organism whose head is constituted by the theological virtues. These animate and inspire the moral virtues from within, to such an extent that they transform the measure of the moral virtues. This led St. Thomas to support the exis-tence of infused moral virtues, needed to proportion the action of the

Christian to the supernatural and theological end to which he is called. Furthermore, he associates with each of the virtues, including the moral virtues, a gift of the Holy Spirit that disposes us to receive divine inspirations that empower us to act according to a higher measure. This is shown in the exposition on the evangelical Beatitudes, which are attained differently according to whether they are attained through the virtues or through the gifts.[13]

Aquinas's understanding of the importance of "infused natural virtues" has implications not only for why ethics must be theological but also for how we should understand the relation of church and world. I am accused, for example, of being a "sectarian, fideistic tribalist" because I argue that the first task of the church is not to make the world more just but to make the world the world. Such a claim, however, is but a correlative of Aquinas's understanding of charity as the form of the virtues. The church, whose holiness is constituted by the confession of sin, must be for the world the redemption that Christ has enacted for the world but that the world has chosen not to embrace.

My identification with the work of John Howard Yoder, and in particular with his anti-Constantinianism, is no doubt one of the reasons that some label me a "sectarian." However, such a label not only fails to rightly understand Yoder's critique of Constantinianism, but also betrays an accommodation to the status quo that itself requires justification. Ironically I am anything but a "sectarian." If I am anything I am a theocrat. I find it very hard to rule nonviolently, but I am willing to try.

The Christocentric and ecclesial focus of my work means I have found it increasingly useful to shape how I do ethics through the liturgy of the church. Accordingly, I think the book that comes closest to representing my work is one I did not write. *The Blackwell Companion to Christian Ethics*, a book I edited with Sam Wells, is, I think, the book people have thought I should write. Instead, I got my friends to write it for me. The essays in the book are ordered according to the liturgy in the hope that readers of the book will be able to see the connections between the common acts of worship and how we must be formed to rightly think of questions of racial reconciliation, beauty, poverty, and practical rationality.

The liturgical and ecclesial focus of my work does, however, raise what many consider a troubling issue, namely, from what ecclesial tradition I write. I am a Methodist who is a communicant at the Church of the Holy Family (Episcopal). Yet I have never written as a Methodist or Episcopalian. My only defense for my ambiguous ecclesial status is that provided by Robert Jenson in the preface to the first volume of his *Systematic Theology*. Jenson observes that to live in a divided church means we must live in radical self-contradiction, and this is particularly true for theology. Jenson writes that though readers may speak of such things as "Roman Catholic" or "Baptist" theology—seemingly harmless enough descriptions—any theologian who described his or her work as "Lutheran" or "Reformed" would deny the name of the church to all and thus betray the theological enterprise. According to Jenson theological work must be "deliberately done in anticipation of the one true church, and this will be throughout apparent, in its use of authorities and its modes of argument."[14] I do not pretend to have always exemplified Jenson's statement of the way the theologian must work, but I have certainly desired so to do.

I hope this romp through "my work" is helpful to introduce at least some of the interrelated themes I have tried to develop. Missing from the account I have tried to provide, however, is the primary agenda that has shaped my work. For at the heart of my work has been an attempt to do theology in a manner that helps Christian and non-Christian alike to understand what it might mean to say what Christians believe is true. To that end I have tried to display how theological convictions work to help us see truthfully the way things are, to suggest how Christians must live if in fact we are to be adequate witnesses to the God we worship. Put negatively, I have always hoped my work might exhibit Cardinal Suhard's claim: "To be a witness does not consist in engaging in propaganda nor even stirring people up, but in being a living mystery. It means to live in such a way that one's life would not make sense if God did not exist."

I confess that I do not think my early work was sufficiently scriptural. Better put, I do not think that my work was appropriately exegetical. But as I approach the last years of my life and work I am happy to say that

155

God has dragged me kicking and screaming back to a concrete engagement with Scripture. Thus my book *Cross-Shattered Christ: Meditations on the Seven Last Words*, as well as the commentary I have just finished on the Gospel of Matthew. I should like to think that the work I have been doing over the years prepared me to write these books. For it is surely the case that the way I have tried to teach myself to do theology requires that theology be done exegetically.

Toward the end of *Transforming Fate into Destiny*, Wells provides what he characterizes as the positive proposals of my theological ethics. I end this account of my work by quoting Wells's first two theses on what he takes to be the heart of my work. I do so because I hope he is right that these two theses are the center of what I have tried to do, because they characterize my deepest theological convictions. Wells observes:

> 1. Stanley Hauerwas believes in the *holy God* who has revealed himself through the patriarchs, through Moses and the Exodus, through the joys and struggles of Israel, through Jesus and the coming of the Spirit, and through the Church. He believes in the sovereignty of this God, in the way God rules through creation, providence and coming *eschaton*, in the definitive way God shows the character of his kingdom, the crucifixion and resurrection of Jesus Christ. Hauerwas also recognizes that the creation is not all that it was intended to be, that sin has infected the world to such a degree that, even after the coming of the Son of God, human projects are invariably subject to pride, jealousy and fear.
>
> 2. Hauerwas maintains that the holy character of the God of Jews and Christians is not self-evident from the workings of nature or the moral law in the human heart or the collective yearnings of humankind. Instead, it is revealed in a *holy story*, the story of Israel, Jesus, and the Church, begun in Scriptures and developed through the history of the Church. From this story Christians learn that God is revealed through human contingency. This means that human contingency is the location for understanding both the character of God and the nature of human response. The way Jesus went to the cross, despite the pressing demands that the world be saved some other way, is the definitive part of the holy story.[15]

That is pretty much it. That is what I think or at least tried to think. I hope it is what the church thinks.

Notes

I am often asked how and why I write so much. No doubt there are a number of explanations, some unknown to me. Work habits surely matter. Writing has become a habit, and hopefully a good one. I am sure one of the reasons I seem to write more than many care to read is because I am a reader. Reading fuels the imagination and forces expression. Because I read, it seems I have something to say—and so I write.

Sermons are first and foremost an oral performance, but they are also a form of writing. So what I read makes a difference for what I preach. Many of you kind enough to read this book have discovered the sermons often refer to books I have read. I have not provided footnotes because I think footnotes in a sermon can not only become pretentious, but more importantly they betray the character of the work the sermon is meant to do. Sermons are one of the few places I think it appropriate to say what another has said without attribution because what another has said cannot be understood as "theirs," but rather belongs to the whole church.

However, I should like to share with the reader some of the writers and their books which have shaped these sermons. This is not an exhaustive list; it is an offering to any reader who might like to read some of the writers who have been important for my thinking and writing—which turns out to be the same thing.

Thomas Aquinas, *Summa Theologica*

W. H. Auden, *Collected Poems*

Augustine, *Confessions*, *The City of God*

Karl Barth, *Church Dogmatics*, *The Dogmatics in Outline*

Jana Bennett, *Water Is Thicker than Blood*

Wendell Berry, *Andy Catlett: Early Travels*

C. H. Dodd, *The Parables*

Gerard Manley Hopkins, *The Poems of Gerard Manley Hopkins*

Robert Jenson, *Systematic Theology*

Herbert McCabe, OP, *God Matters*

Reinhold Niebuhr, *Love and Justice*

John Paul II, *Crossing the Threshold of Hope*

Timothy Radcliff, OP, *Seven Last Words*

Gene Rogers, *After the Spirit*

Robert Wilken, *The Spirit of Early Christian Thought*

Rowan Williams, *Grace and Necessity: Reflections on Art and Love*

Ludwig Wittgenstein, *Tractatus Logico-Philosophicus*, *The Philosophical Investigations*

John Howard Yoder, *The Politics of Jesus*, *For the Nations*

Introduction

1. For my account of the relation or lack of relation between theology and the modern university, see *The State of the University: Academic Knowledges and the Knowledge of God* (Oxford: Blackwell, 2007).

2. In the preface to his *Forty-Four Sermons* (London: Epworth, 1964), John Wesley claims he has designed his sermons to be "plain truth for plain people." Accordingly, he tried to avoid philosophical speculations, perplexed and intricate reasonings, and "even the show of learning." Yet Wesley acknowledges he may "sometimes slide into them unaware" (p. v). I take Wesley's claim to write plain truth for plain people to be a wonderful rhetorical device to entice his reader to agree with his sermons. Who would not desire to be a "plain person" capable of understanding "plain truth"? I have not tried to imagine my ideal reader one way or the other. These sermons are quite simply written the way they are because that is the way I write.

3. Karl Barth, *Deliverance to the Captives* (New York: Harper and Row, 1959), 8. For a wonderful exploration of Barth on preaching, as well as the exemplification of what such preaching might look like, see William Willimon, *Conversations with Barth on Preaching* (Nashville: Abingdon, 2006).

4. Barth, *Deliverance to the Captives*, 9.

5. For an explanation of why I think you should never try to explain, see my "Explaining Why Willimon Never Explains," in *Disrupting Time: Sermons, Prayers, and Sundries* (Eugene, OR: Cascade Books, 2004), 224–33.

6. Charles Taylor, *A Secular Age* (Cambridge: Harvard University Press, 2007), 3.

7. Jonathan Lear, *Radical Hope: Ethics in the Face of Cultural Devastation* (Cambridge: Harvard University Press, 2006).

8. Ibid., 2.

9. Ibid., 6.

10. Ibid., 56.

11. See John Howard Yoder's important chapter, "'But we do see Jesus': The Particularity of Incarnation and the Universality of Truth," in *The Priestly Kingdom: Social Ethics as Gospel*, with a foreword by Stanley Hauerwas (Notre Dame, IN: University of Notre Dame Press, 2001), 46–62.

12. John Howard Yoder, *Preface to Theology: Christology and Theological Method*, with an introduction by Stanley Hauerwas and Alex Sider (Grand Rapids: Brazos, 2002), 41.

13. Ibid., 228.

14. Yoder observes that words are to be tested by whether they coincide with Christ. Thus in 1 John 4 they are tested by their appropriate or inappropriate affirmation of the incarnation and in 1 Corinthians 12 by how they fit with the affirmation that "Jesus Christ is Lord." Which means, according to Yoder, "as the church continues to meet new challenges, speak new languages, and enter new cultures in the leading of the Holy Spirit, she always makes new statements she claims are true, but then they have to be tested. They are tested by their link to the core message, the Jesus story. Then they are tested by their relationship to the wider body of primitive traditions, like the Gospels. Then they can begin to be tested by the way the New Testament church read the Old Testament, looking behind itself to find its face there" (Ibid., 379–80).

15. Ibid., 371.

16. Reinhold Niebuhr, *Leaves from the Notebooks of a Tamed Cynic* (New York: Living Age Books, 1957), 128.

17. For my extended reflections on this understanding of war, see "Sacrificing the Sacrifices of War," *Criswell Theological Review* 4, no. 2 (Spring 2007): 77–96.

18. Marilyn Chandler McEntyre, "Power Line," *Christian Century* 125, no. 18 (September 9, 2008): 30–35.

19. John Howard Yoder, *He Came Preaching Peace* (Scottsdale, PA: Herald, 1985), 12.

20. It is my strong conviction that there is an essential connection between good preaching and Christian orthodoxy because there is a strong connection between Christian doctrine and right living. For a wonderful collection of sermons illustrative of these claims, see Ben Quash and Michael Wards, eds. *Heresies and How to Avoid Them: Why It Matters What Christians Believe* (London: SPCK, 2007). In the book's foreword I suggest that the Christian reading of the Bible is a delicate task, as complex and beautiful as a spider's web. But spiders' webs are fragile, requiring constant repair, which means that in the process of repair connections are revealed that had not been anticipated. There is an order to orthodoxy that is beautiful and fragile—beautiful because of its fragility. For a similar view of the work doctrine should do, see Kevin Vanhoozer, *The Drama of Doctrine: A Canonical-Linguistic Approach to Christian Theology* (Louisville: Westminster John Knox, 2005). For those who care about such matters it will be apparent that I do not share Vanhoozer's criticisms of George Lindbeck.

21. See, for example, John Yoder's account of why we need to speak of atonement but why in doing so we must make articulate the relationship between Jesus's proclamation of the kingdom, his forgiving people, his teaching people, his making of people a church, and his sending people into mission. Yoder suggests that the Pauline understanding of our union with Christ rightly makes it impossible to avoid the nonresistant character of God's reconciling love necessary to maintain the difference between church and world as the best expression of atonement (*Preface to Theology*, 305–13).

22. See, for example, my essay, "Reflections on the 'Appeal to Abolish War,' " in *Between Poetry and Politics: Essays in Honour of Enda McDonagh*, ed. Linda Hogan and Barbara FitzGerald (Dublin, UK: Columba Press, 2003), 135–47.

23. For a sermon that does address directly the American response to September 11, 2001, see my *Performing the Faith: Bonhoeffer and the Practice of Nonviolence* (Grand Rapids: Brazos, 2004), 211–14.

Chapter 2 Blinded by the Light

1. The Rt. Rev. Macleord Baker Ochola II, retired bishop of the diocese of Kitgum in northern Uganda, arrived in Chapel Hill on September 14, 2005. He served as bishop-in-residence at the Church of the Holy Family, licensed by the bishop of North Carolina to preach, to celebrate the Holy Eucharist, and to otherwise perform priestly functions, from September 26, 2005, until October 19, 2005, when the rector, the Rev. Timothy E. Kimbrough, returned from a sabbatical leave. Bishop Ochola continued his visit at Holy Family with occasional speaking engagements both here and elsewhere through March 19, 2006.

Chapter 3 So Much Depends

1. "The Ekklesia Project is a network of Christians from across the Christian tradition who rejoice in a peculiar kind of friendship rooted in our common love of God and the Church" (www.ekklesiaproject.org).

Chapter 8 A Cross-Shattered Church

1. Richard Hays is the George Washington Ivey Professor of New Testament in the Divinity School at Duke University.

Chapter 14 A Deadly Business

1. Son and daughter of Richard and Kristy Church. Richard is a former graduate student of mine.

Chapter 15 To Be Made Human

1. Daughter of former student Gary Eichelberger.

Chapter 16 Water Is Thicker than Blood

1. Jana is a former graduate student.

Chapter 17 Anointing Grace

1. Grace is a former Duke Divinity School student.

Appendix

1. Originally published as "Matthew: Making the Familiar Strange," *Homily Service* 31, no. 1 (December 1, 2007): 2–4.

2. Originally published in *Journal for Preachers* 31, no. 2 (2008).

3. Samuel Wells, *Transforming Fate into Destiny: The Theological Ethics of Stanley Hauerwas* (Cumbria, UK: Paternoster, 1998).

4. Herbert McCabe, *Law, Love, and Language* (London: Continuum, 2003).

5. Ibid., 86.

6. Ibid., 142.

7. See, for example, Stanley Hauerwas and Romand Coles, *Christianity, Democracy and the Radical Ordinary: Conversations between a Radical Democrat and a Christian* (Eugene, OR: Cascade, 2008).

8. Rowan Williams, *Lost Icons: Reflections on Cultural Bereavement* (Edinburgh: T&T Clark, 2000).

9. Wells, *Transforming Fate into Destiny*, 179.

10. Ibid., 180.

11. Samuel Wells, *Improvisation: The Drama of Christian Ethics* (Grand Rapids: Brazos, 2004), 53–55.

12. John Howard Yoder, *For the Nations: Essays Evangelical and Public* (Grand Rapids: Eerdmans, 1997), 212.

13. Servais Pinckaers, *The Pinckaers Reader: Renewing Thomist Moral Theology*, ed. John Berkman and Craig Steven Titus (Washington, DC: Catholic University of America Press, 2005), 15.

14. Robert Jensen, *Systematic Theology*, vol. 1 (New York: Oxford University Press, 1997), viii.

15. Wells, *Transforming Fate into Destiny*, 126–27.